W9-DGE-173

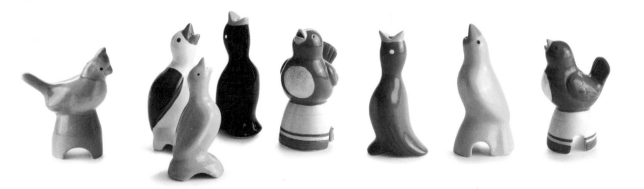

the Southern PIE Book

Oxmoor

*This book is dedicated to my
incredible and amazing children,
Ben, Katie, and Jackson, whom I love with
my entire being. You make my life worth living
and always will. And to three of the most talented
people I have ever had the privilege of working
with, Becky Stayner, Fonda Shaia, and Ana Kelly,
thank you for such glorious images
that make pie a thing of beauty.*

Pie.

The word alone can bring a smile to your face.

In the South, pies are a delectable expression of love. You can't eat a piece of pie that someone has spent an afternoon making without a feeling of genuine devotion for the maker. With one bite you'll know that you have been lovingly fussed over.

When I was growing up, we had pie almost every Sunday in some form or fashion. The most memorable pies are the ones my mama or grandmother made. When I make their recipes, it's almost as if they are right in the kitchen with me. The dearest recipes are handwritten on old recipe cards smudged with vanilla or chocolate. It's a sure sign that they're worth making.

The wonderful thing about pie is that it can be made with a few simple ingredients or with the most decadent combination you can come up with. Either way, it's still delicious. With a little look through the pantry, you can gather the makings of a pie. *The ingredients that I find absolutely essential are shown in "Pure and simple" on page 274.* I am so fascinated by the fact that something so delicious can be made from these humble staples.

The filling is usually the easy part—a few apples, some sugar and spice—but the crust usually causes some hesitation. Whoever said "easy as pie" evidently never made piecrust from scratch. But with a little practice and a rolling pin, you can make pies like an expert. *On pages 32 and 33, I've included step-by-step instructions so you can create perfect lattice crusts and crust edges too.* My grandmother, with a simple motion of her index finger and thumb, could effortlessly make a beautiful crimped design around the edge of the crust, like a crown of glory. To this day, try as I might, I just can't duplicate it.

Before I was old enough to bake, my mother would give me the soft, tattered scraps of dough that were left from trimming the edges. I would roll and shape the scraps into whatever I fancied, which usually ended up as a heart. Meanwhile she would gingerly place the smooth rounds of dough onto the pie plates, dented and worn from frequent use. I've never been too fussy about having the fanciest tools, but some of them just make baking so much easier; *look on page 270 for my favorite pie equipment.*

Once baked, simple pastry dough transforms into a buttery, flaky crust that becomes the foundation for so many wonderful fillings. Sometimes I break from tradition and swap out one crust for another. This simple switch can be such a delightful surprise; *my suggestions for crust and filling pairings can be found in the Crust Index on page 278.*

Just about everyone has a favorite pie. Mine is a creamy, intensely lemony icebox pie made with a generous graham cracker crust and topped with a gracious plenty of just-barely sweetened fresh whipped cream. It is so irresistible to me; I can eat it until there isn't a single crumb left. I might even get annoyed if someone else eats the last piece, even though pie is meant to be shared. Egg custard was my grandmother's pick. I can't make it without thinking of her. Fudgy chocolate pie was by far my mother's favorite. She loved it served warm, topped with vanilla ice cream and gooey fudge sauce, and sprinkled with toasted pecans—or sometimes just plain naked if church ran late.

I hope you find your favorite in this collection of recipes, some of which I've gathered from friends, family, and colleagues. Other classic ones have been passed down for generations. I've added some fun new creations, along with a few surprises. So enjoy, and share the love.

J'adore les tartes, y'all!

Jan Moon

Contents

From the BOTTOM UP

The secret to a perfectly flaky crust is to obey two rules: Be gentle with the dough, and keep the ingredients and the dough cold. Once you master it, you will wonder why you ever doubted yourself.

PIE & TART CRUSTS

Simply Piecrust *12*

Deep South Piecrust *12*

Fried Pie Pastry *15*

Cream Cheese Piecrust *15*

Rustic Almond Piecrust *16*

Cheddar Piecrust *16*

Coconut Piecrust *19*

Lemon Cornmeal Piecrust *19*

Sweet Pastry *20*

Chocolate Pastry *23*

Sandwich Cookie Piecrust *23*

Shortbread Cookie Piecrust *24*

Vanilla Wafer Piecrust *24*

Graham Cracker Piecrust *27*

Gingersnap Piecrust *27*

Pretzel Piecrust *28*

Phyllo Piecrust *31*

Simply Piecrust

MAKES 1 (9-INCH) PIECRUST   **HANDS-ON TIME 8 MIN.**   **TOTAL TIME 1 HR., 37 MIN.**

This is my favorite, foolproof, all-purpose crust!

Ingredients

1¼ cups all-purpose flour

½ cup cold butter, cut into pieces

¼ tsp. table salt

4 to 5 Tbsp. ice water

1. Combine first 3 ingredients in a bowl with a pastry blender until mixture resembles small peas. Sprinkle ice water, 1 Tbsp. at a time, over surface of mixture in bowl; stir with a fork until dry ingredients are moistened. Shape into a ball; cover and chill 30 minutes.

2. Preheat oven to 425°. Roll dough into a 13-inch circle on a lightly floured surface. Fit into a 9-inch pie plate; fold edges under, and crimp.

3. Line pastry with aluminum foil, and fill with pie weights or dried beans. Bake at 425° for 15 minutes. Remove weights and foil; bake 5 to 10 more minutes or until golden brown. Cool completely on a wire rack.

Deep South Piecrust

MAKES 1 (9-INCH) PIECRUST   **HANDS-ON TIME 5 MIN.**   **TOTAL TIME 2 HR., 5 MIN.**

When you want a super-flaky, richly flavored crust, use lard—it doesn't get more Southern than that!

Ingredients

1¼ cups all-purpose flour

¼ cup cold butter, cut into pieces

¼ cup cold lard, cut into pieces

¼ tsp. table salt

3 Tbsp. ice water

1. Combine first 4 ingredients in a bowl with a pastry blender until mixture resembles small peas. Sprinkle ice water, 1 Tbsp. at a time, over surface of mixture in bowl; stir with a fork until dry ingredients are moistened. Shape into a ball; cover and chill 30 minutes.

2. Preheat oven to 425°. Roll dough into a 13-inch circle on a lightly floured surface. Fit into a 9-inch pie plate; fold edges under, and crimp.

3. Line pastry with aluminum foil, and fill with pie weights or dried beans. Bake at 425° for 15 minutes. Remove weights and foil; bake 5 to 10 more minutes or until golden brown. Cool completely on a wire rack.

How to Make
Dough in a Food Processor

Pulse *flour* and *salt* in a food processor
3 or 4 times or until combined. Add *butter*,
and pulse 5 or 6 times or until crumbly. With
processor running, gradually add *water*, 1 Tbsp.
at a time, and process until dough forms a
ball and pulls away from sides of bowl,
adding more water if necessary.
Cover and chill 30 minutes.

Fried Pie Pastry

Fried Pie Pastry

MAKES 14 FRIED PIES   **HANDS-ON TIME 6 MIN.**   **TOTAL TIME 1 HR., 6 MIN.**

Fried pies need a little egg to hold it all together. I use this crust for all my fried pies.

1. Combine flour and salt in a bowl; cut in shortening with a pastry blender until crumbly. Combine egg, 4 Tbsp. ice water, and vinegar; add to flour mixture, stirring until dough forms a ball and pulls away from sides of bowl, adding more water if necessary.

2. Shape into a disk; cover and chill at least 1 hour or until ready to use.

Ingredients

3 cups all-purpose flour

1 tsp. table salt

¾ cup cold shortening

1 large egg,
lightly beaten

4 to 6 Tbsp. ice water

1 tsp. white vinegar

Cream Cheese Piecrust

MAKES 1 (9-INCH) PIECRUST   **HANDS-ON TIME 14 MIN.**   **TOTAL TIME 2 HR., 14 MIN.**

This is a great pastry for beginners. It's soft, easy to work with, and very forgiving.

1. Beat first 4 ingredients at medium speed with an electric mixer until creamy. Gradually add flour, beating at low speed just until blended. Add ice water, beating until mixture forms a ball and pulls away from sides of bowl.

2. Shape into a disk; cover and chill 1 hour.

3. Preheat oven to 400°. Roll dough to ¼-inch thickness on a lightly floured surface. Fit into a 9-inch pie plate; fold edges under, and crimp. Freeze 10 minutes or until firm.

4. Bake at 400° for 10 to 12 minutes or until light golden brown. Remove from oven to a wire rack, and cool completely (about 30 minutes).

Ingredients

6 Tbsp. butter,
at room temperature

2 oz. cream cheese,
at room temperature

2 Tbsp. sugar

¼ tsp. table salt

1¼ cups all-purpose
flour

1½ Tbsp. ice water

Rustic Almond Piecrust

MAKES 1 (9-INCH) PIECRUST   **HANDS-ON TIME 30 MIN.**   **TOTAL TIME 2 HR., 15 MIN.**

Ingredients

1 cup all-purpose flour

½ cup whole
natural almonds
(with skin), toasted

2½ Tbsp. dark
brown sugar

¼ tsp. table salt

⅛ tsp. ground cinnamon

6 Tbsp. cold butter,
cut into pieces

3 Tbsp. ice water

1. Pulse first 5 ingredients in a food processor 2 or 3 times or until coarsely chopped. Add butter; pulse 3 times or until crumbly. With processor running, gradually add ice water, and process until dough forms a ball and pulls away from sides of bowl. Shape into a ball; cover and chill 1 hour.

2. Preheat oven to 375°. Roll dough into an 11-inch circle on a lightly floured surface. Fit into a 9-inch pie plate; fold edges under, and crimp.

3. Bake at 375° for 15 minutes. Remove from oven to a wire rack, and cool completely (about 30 minutes).

Cheddar Piecrust

MAKES 1 (9-INCH) PIECRUST   **HANDS-ON TIME 10 MIN.**   **TOTAL TIME 1 HR., 40 MIN.**

*Pair this remarkable crust with sweet or savory fillings.
I love it with fruit fillings or summer tomatoes.*

Ingredients

1¼ cups all-purpose
flour

⅓ cup cold butter,
cut into pieces

½ tsp. table salt

¾ cup (3 oz.)
shredded white
Cheddar cheese

4 to 5 Tbsp. ice water

1. Combine first 3 ingredients in a bowl with a pastry blender until mixture resembles small peas. Stir in cheese. Sprinkle ice water, 1 Tbsp. at a time, over surface of mixture in bowl; stir with a fork until dry ingredients are moistened. Shape into a ball; cover and chill 30 minutes.

2. Preheat oven to 425°. Roll dough into a 13-inch circle on a lightly floured surface. Fit into a 9-inch pie plate; fold edges under, and crimp.

3. Line pastry with aluminum foil, and fill with pie weights or dried beans. Bake at 425° for 15 minutes. Remove weights and foil; bake 5 to 10 more minutes or until golden brown. Remove from oven to a wire rack, and cool completely (about 30 minutes).

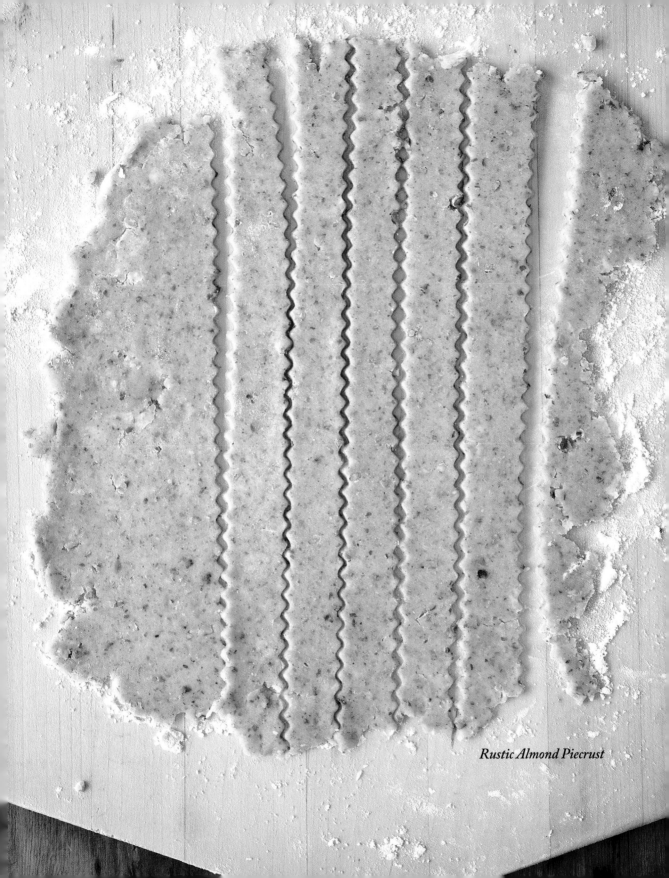

Rustic Almond Piecrust

Coconut Piecrust

Coconut Piecrust

MAKES 1 (9-INCH) PIECRUST   HANDS-ON TIME 5 MIN.   TOTAL TIME 1 HR., 5 MIN.

I love how easy this crust is—you don't need a rolling pin, just press it into the pan!

1. Preheat oven to 350°. Stir together first 4 ingredients in a large bowl. Add butter; stir until blended. Firmly press into a 9-inch pie plate. Chill 30 minutes.

2. Bake at 350° for 8 minutes or until crust is golden. Remove from oven to a wire rack, and cool completely (about 20 minutes).

Ingredients

1½ cups sweetened flaked coconut

6 Tbsp. graham cracker crumbs

2 Tbsp. sugar

1 Tbsp. all-purpose flour

4 Tbsp. butter, melted

Lemon Cornmeal Piecrust

MAKES 1 (9-INCH) PIECRUST   HANDS-ON TIME 12 MIN.   TOTAL TIME 1 HR., 42 MIN.

The unexpected crunch of the cornmeal paired with a bright hint of lemon is just heavenly.

1. Stir together first 5 ingredients in a medium bowl; cut in butter with a pastry blender until crumbly. Sprinkle ice water, 1 Tbsp. at a time, over surface of mixture in bowl; stir with a fork until dry ingredients are moistened. Shape into a disk; cover and chill 30 minutes.

2. Preheat oven to 400°. Roll dough to ¼-inch thickness on a lightly floured surface. Fit into a 9-inch pie plate; fold edges under, and crimp. Freeze 10 minutes or until firm.

3. Line pastry with aluminum foil, and fill with pie weights or dried beans. Bake at 400° for 15 minutes. Remove weights and foil; bake 5 more minutes or until light golden brown. Remove from oven to a wire rack, and cool completely (about 30 minutes).

Ingredients

¾ cup all-purpose flour

½ cup plain white cornmeal

⅓ cup powdered sugar

1 Tbsp. lemon zest

¼ tsp. table salt

½ cup cold butter, cut into pieces

⅓ cup ice water

Sweet Pastry

MAKES 1 (10-INCH) TART CRUST   HANDS-ON TIME 9 MIN.   TOTAL TIME 1 HR., 46 MIN.

When I make tarts, this is my go-to crust—its buttery, cookie-like texture is such a treat.

Ingredients

½ cup butter, softened

¼ cup sugar

1½ cups all-purpose flour

½ tsp. table salt

2 large egg yolks

1. Beat butter and sugar at medium speed with an electric mixer until fluffy. Add flour and salt; beat at low speed just until combined. Add egg yolks and 1 Tbsp. water; beat at low speed until dough forms a ball and pulls away from sides of bowl. Shape into a 7-inch log. Cover, and chill 1 hour.

2. Preheat oven to 400°. Cut dough log into ¼-inch-thick slices; arrange slices in a single layer over bottom and up sides of a 10-inch tart pan with removable bottom. Press slices together, and press into fluted edges. Fold any excess dough over outside of pan, and pinch to secure to pan. (This will keep dough from sliding down pan as it bakes.) Prick dough generously with a fork.

3. Bake at 400° for 17 minutes or until lightly browned. Remove from oven to a wire rack, and cool completely (about 20 minutes).

Tip *This soft and crumbly pastry is really a shortbread cookie dough, so instead of rolling it, just press it into the pan.*

Chocolate Pastry

Chocolate Pastry

MAKES 1 (10-INCH) TART CRUST   HANDS-ON TIME **10 MIN.**   TOTAL TIME **1 HR., 57 MIN.**

1. Whisk together first 4 ingredients in a medium bowl until blended. Add butter, and gently rub with fingers until mixture resembles fine meal. Add egg, stirring with a fork just until dry ingredients are moistened and dough can be shaped into a ball. Flatten ball into a disk; cover and chill 1 hour.

2. Preheat oven to 400°. Roll dough into a 12-inch circle on a lightly floured surface. Fit piecrust into a 10-inch tart pan with removable bottom; press into fluted edges. Fold any excess dough over outside of pan, and pinch to secure to pan. (This will keep piecrust from sliding down pan as it bakes.) Freeze 10 minutes or until firm.

3. Bake at 400° for 17 minutes or until set. Remove from oven to a wire rack, and cool completely (about 20 minutes).

Ingredients

1 cup all-purpose flour

¾ cup powdered sugar

⅓ cup unsweetened cocoa

⅛ tsp. table salt

½ cup butter, cut into pieces

1 large egg, lightly beaten

Sandwich Cookie Piecrust

MAKES 1 (9-INCH) PIECRUST   HANDS-ON TIME **3 MIN.**   TOTAL TIME **43 MIN.**

My granddaughter loves to help crush the cookies in a zip-top plastic bag if we decide not to use a food processor.

1. Preheat oven to 350°. Process cookie pieces in a food processor until cookies are finely crushed. With processor running, pour butter through food chute; pulse 4 or 5 times, just until blended.

2. Firmly press crumb mixture into a 9-inch pie plate. Bake at 350° for 10 minutes. Remove from oven to a wire rack, and cool completely (about 30 minutes).

Ingredients

18 cream-filled chocolate or vanilla sandwich cookies, broken

3 Tbsp. butter, melted

Shortbread Cookie Piecrust

MAKES 1 (9-INCH) PIECRUST   HANDS-ON TIME 4 MIN.   TOTAL TIME 44 MIN.

You can use almost any cookie in this crust, but shortbread cookies are a classic.

Ingredients

1 (7.25-oz.) package
shortbread cookies

2 Tbsp. sugar

¼ cup butter,
melted

1. Preheat oven to 350°. Process cookies in a food processor 30 seconds to measure 1⅔ cups fine crumbs. Add sugar; pulse 3 times. With processor running, pour butter through food chute; process until blended.

2. Press crumb mixture into a 9-inch pie plate.

3. Bake at 350° for 10 minutes or until lightly browned. Remove from oven to a wire rack, and cool completely (about 30 minutes).

Note: We tested with Pepperidge Farm Chessmen cookies.

Vanilla Wafer Piecrust

MAKES 1 (9-INCH) PIECRUST   HANDS-ON TIME 10 MIN.   TOTAL TIME 50 MIN.

This rich buttery crust is so good you'll want to make a pie just to have the crust.

Ingredients

54 vanilla wafers

2 Tbsp. sugar

⅛ tsp. table salt

¼ cup butter,
melted

1. Preheat oven to 350°. Process cookies in a food processor 30 seconds to measure 1½ cups fine crumbs. Add sugar and salt; pulse 3 times. With processor running, pour butter through food chute; process until blended.

2. Press crumb mixture into a 9-inch pie plate.

3. Bake at 350° for 10 to 12 minutes or until golden brown. Remove from oven to a wire rack, and cool completely (about 30 minutes).

Shortbread Cookie Piecrust

Graham Cracker Piecrust

Graham Cracker Piecrust

MAKES 1 (9-INCH) PIECRUST   HANDS-ON TIME **10 MIN.**   TOTAL TIME **50 MIN.**

1. Preheat oven to 350°. Stir together all ingredients in a medium bowl. Press crumb mixture into a 9-inch pie plate.

2. Bake at 350° for 10 to 12 minutes or until lightly browned. Remove from oven to a wire rack, and cool completely (about 30 minutes).

Variation: Peanut-Graham Cracker Piecrust
Prepare recipe as directed, substituting **1 cup graham cracker crumbs** and **½ cup finely chopped peanuts** for the 1½ cups graham cracker crumbs.

Ingredients

1½ cups graham cracker crumbs

6 Tbsp. butter, melted

3 Tbsp. sugar

Gingersnap Piecrust

MAKES 1 (9-INCH) PIECRUST   HANDS-ON TIME **6 MIN.**   TOTAL TIME **46 MIN.**

Slightly spicy, gingersnaps add a special zing to the piecrust. It's the perfect companion for creamy pie fillings.

1. Preheat oven to 350°. Process gingersnaps in a food processor 30 seconds to measure 1½ cups fine crumbs. Add sugar; pulse 3 times. With processor running, pour butter through food chute; process until blended.

2. Press crumb mixture into a 9-inch pie plate. Bake at 350° for 8 to 10 minutes or until lightly browned. Remove from oven to a wire rack, and cool completely (about 30 minutes).

Variation: Gingersnap-Graham Cracker Piecrust
Prepare recipe as directed, substituting **14 gingersnaps** and **6 graham crackers** for the 28 gingersnaps.

Ingredients

28 gingersnaps

2 Tbsp. sugar

6 Tbsp. butter, melted

Pretzel Piecrust

MAKES 1 (9-INCH) PIECRUST **HANDS-ON TIME 4 MIN.** **TOTAL TIME 44 MIN.**

There is something so tantalizing about the salty-sweet combination of a pretzel crust. This sturdy crust holds its own next to a rich, heavy filling.

Ingredients

2½ cups pretzel sticks (about 4 oz.)

2 Tbsp. dark brown sugar

½ cup butter, melted

1. Preheat oven to 350°. Process pretzels in a food processor to measure 1¼ cups fine crumbs. Add sugar; pulse 3 times until blended. With processor running, pour butter through food chute; process just until blended.

2. Press crumb mixture into a lightly greased 9-inch pie plate. Bake at 350° for 10 to 12 minutes or until lightly browned. Remove from oven to a wire rack, and cool completely (about 30 minutes).

Tip *To give this crust a modern look, try using a 9-inch deep-dish fluted tart pan.*

Phyllo Piecrust

MAKES 1 (9-INCH) PIECRUST   HANDS-ON TIME 11 MIN.   TOTAL TIME 56 MIN.

Working with phyllo dough is actually pretty easy, as long as you are prepared. Let frozen phyllo thaw in the refrigerator for a few hours and up to overnight—no longer! Then unroll the dough, and keep it covered with a barely damp towel. Work with one sheet at a time, and use lots of butter!

1. Preheat oven to 350°. Place 1 phyllo sheet on a large cutting board or work surface. (Keep remaining phyllo covered with a damp towel to prevent drying out.) Lightly brush with melted butter, and place in a lightly greased 9-inch pie plate; sprinkle with ½ tsp. sugar. (Phyllo will hang over edge of pan.) Repeat with remaining phyllo sheets, butter, and sugar, turning sheets as they are stacked to cover pie plate. Quickly fold edges under, pressing gently to form edge of crust. (Phyllo dries out quickly.)

2. Bake at 350° for 15 minutes or until golden brown. Remove from oven to a wire rack, and cool completely (about 30 minutes).

Ingredients

12 frozen phyllo sheets, thawed

6 Tbsp. butter, melted

2 Tbsp. sugar

lattice crust

Lattices have the crunch of a double crust but let you see the filling bubbling inside.

TRADITIONAL Cut dough into 9 (1-inch-wide) strips. Weave strips in a lattice design over filling, leaving ½-inch space between strips. Gently press ends of strips into bottom crust; crimp edge of crust.

TIGHT Cut dough into 16 (½-inch-wide) strips. Weave strips in a lattice design over filling, leaving as little space as possible between strips. Gently press ends of strips into bottom crust; crimp edge of crust.

IRREGULAR Cut dough into 10 to 15 strips of varying sizes. Weave strips in a lattice design over filling, leaving ½-inch to 1-inch space between strips. Gently press ends of strips into bottom crust; crimp edge of crust.

CUTOUT DOUBLE Using a small cookie cutter, cut out 6 to 10 shapes from dough center. Place dough over filling; fold edges under, sealing to bottom crust, and crimp as desired. Place cutouts over crust, if desired.

crust edge

An extra-special crust can make a simple pie fit for a celebration!

BRAID Make ½ recipe additional piecrust. Divide dough into 3 equal portions, and roll into thin long ropes. Flatten ropes into ribbons, and braid. Use water to adhere braid to crust edge.

SIMPLE FLUTE Fold edges under, and flute edges using the thumb and forefinger of one hand to form the dough around the thumb of the other hand. Repeat around crust edge.

PEARL Make ½ recipe additional piecrust. Cut into small pieces, and roll into ¼-inch balls. Press them to adhere, one by one around crust edge, brushing with water as needed.

CUTOUTS Make ½ recipe additional piecrust. Cut out small shapes using a small cookie cutter. Brush crust edge with water, and lay cutouts overlapping around edge, pressing to adhere.

LEAFY VINE Using kitchen shears, make ½-inch diagonal cuts all around crust edge, spacing them ½ inch apart. Press every other tab toward center of pie.

FORK-PRESS Fold edges under, and press dough with the tines of a fork. Repeat around crust edge.

Truly
SOUTHERN

In the South, recipes are treasured pieces
    of history that are as valuable as any heirloom.
Some are freely shared and others guarded
    like family secrets; these are my most beloved.

CLASSIC SOUTHERN PIES

Sweet Buttermilk Pie *36*

Amelia's Egg Custard Pie *39*

Old-Time Vinegar Pie *40*

Tart Lemon Chess Pie *43*

Maple Chess Pie *with* Brown Sugar Bacon *44*

Shoofly Pie *47*

Fresh Pumpkin Pie *48*

Chocolate Fudge Pie *with* Praline Crumble *51*

Down South Muscadine Pie *52*

Virginia Peanut Pie *55*

Maple *and* Black Walnut Pie *56*

Billie's Holiday Pie *59*

Sweet Buttermilk Pie

MAKES 8 SERVINGS HANDS-ON TIME 21 MIN. TOTAL TIME 3 HR., 26 MIN.

Buttermilk pie has stood the test of time because it's that perfect balance of the soft tang of buttermilk with just enough sweetness.

1. Prepare Simply Piecrust as directed, baking in a 9-inch pie plate. Reduce oven temperature to 350°.

2. Whisk together sugar and flour in a large bowl. Add eggs, 1 at a time, whisking just until blended after each addition. Whisk in buttermilk and next 4 ingredients. Pour into prepared crust.

3. Bake at 350° for 35 minutes or until center barely moves when pie plate is touched, shielding edges with aluminum foil to prevent excessive browning. Serve warm or chilled with Whipped Cream.

Ingredients

— 1 —
SIMPLY PIECRUST
p. 12

plus

1 cup sugar

2½ Tbsp. all-purpose flour

4 large eggs

1 cup buttermilk

3 Tbsp. butter, melted

1 tsp. lemon zest

1 Tbsp. fresh lemon juice

1 tsp. vanilla extract

Whipped Cream
(p. 256)

Amelia's Egg Custard Pie

MAKES 8 SERVINGS   HANDS-ON TIME 10 MIN.   TOTAL TIME 2 HR., 25 MIN.

My grandmother Amelia loved this pie. She would always make it for me when I was little. When she became too old to bake anymore, I would make it for her.

1. Prepare Simply Piecrust through step 2 in a 9-inch pie plate.

2. Preheat oven to 350°. Beat eggs and next 4 ingredients at medium speed with an electric mixer until blended. Stir in milk and whipping cream; pour into prepared crust. Sprinkle with nutmeg.

3. Bake at 350° for 45 minutes or until a knife inserted 1 inch from edge of pie comes out clean. Remove from oven to a wire rack, and cool 1 hour. Serve warm, at room temperature, or cover pie, and chill until ready to serve.

Above and beyond Look on page 33 to find new ideas for making beautiful crust edges. Follow the "braid" instructions to mirror the pie at left.

Ingredients

— 1 —
SIMPLY PIECRUST

p. 12

plus

8 large egg yolks

1 cup sugar

2 Tbsp. butter, melted

1 tsp. vanilla extract

⅛ tsp. table salt

1 cup milk

1 cup whipping cream

¼ tsp. freshly grated nutmeg

Old-Time Vinegar Pie

MAKES 8 SERVINGS   **HANDS-ON TIME 10 MIN.**   **TOTAL TIME 3 HR.**

Born from hard times, vinegar takes the place of milk or cream, creating this unpretentious pie that remains a favorite at Southern down-home dinners.

1. Prepare Simply Piecrust through step 2 in a 9-inch pie plate.

2. Preheat oven to 350°. Whisk together eggs and next 4 ingredients. Pour into prepared crust.

3. Bake at 350° for 50 minutes or until set. Remove from oven to a wire rack, and cool completely (about 2 hours).

Tip *Be sure to cook this pie until it is set. When it is completely baked, the filling will turn a golden brown.*

Ingredients

— 1 —
SIMPLY
PIECRUST

p. 12

plus

4 large eggs,
lightly beaten

1½ cups sugar

½ cup butter,
melted

3 Tbsp. apple cider
vinegar or
white vinegar

1 tsp. vanilla extract

Tart Lemon Chess Pie

MAKES 8 SERVINGS   HANDS-ON TIME 23 MIN.   TOTAL TIME 3 HR., 8 MIN.

The robust flavor from freshly squeezed lemons is outstanding. It's well worth the effort to zest and juice fresh ones to achieve that pure and clean citrus punch.

1. Prepare Simply Piecrust as directed, baking in a 9-inch pie plate. Reduce oven temperature to 350°.

2. Whisk together sugar and next 6 ingredients in a large bowl. Add eggs, whisking until blended. Pour into prepared crust.

3. Bake at 350° for 45 minutes or until pie is set, shielding edges with aluminum foil to prevent excessive browning. Remove from oven to a wire rack, and cool completely (about 1 hour).

Ingredients

— 1 —
SIMPLY
PIECRUST

p. 12

plus

1½ cups sugar

2 tsp. lemon zest

¾ cup fresh lemon juice
(about 3 lemons)

½ cup butter,
melted

1½ Tbsp. cornstarch

1 Tbsp. plain
yellow cornmeal

¼ tsp. table salt

4 large eggs

Maple Chess Pie
with Brown Sugar Bacon

MAKES 8 SERVINGS   HANDS-ON TIME 21 MIN.   TOTAL TIME 3 HR., 55 MIN.

One bite of this rich maple and brown sugar pie combined with the caramelized salty-sweet bacon will make your taste buds sing for joy.

1. Prepare Deep South Piecrust as directed, baking in a 9-inch pie plate. Reduce oven temperature to 400°.

2. Prepare Brown Sugar Bacon. Reduce oven temperature to 350°.

3. Whisk together maple sugar and next 7 ingredients in a large bowl until blended. Add eggs, whisking until well blended. Pour filling into prepared crust.

4. Bake at 350° for 45 minutes or until set, shielding edges with aluminum foil to prevent excessive browning. Remove from oven to a wire rack, and cool completely (1 hour).

5. Serve with Whipped Cream and crumbled Brown Sugar Bacon.

Brown Sugar Bacon

Preheat oven to 400°. Dredge **6 thick bacon slices** in **¼ cup firmly packed dark brown sugar,** pressing to adhere. Place bacon in a single layer on a lightly greased wire rack in an aluminum foil-lined jelly-roll pan. Bake at 400° for 25 to 29 minutes or until browned and almost crisp. Cool completely on wire rack (about 30 minutes). Bacon will continue to crisp as it cools. Coarsely crumble bacon.

Ingredients

— 1 —
DEEP
SOUTH
PIECRUST
p.12

plus

Brown Sugar Bacon

1 cup maple sugar

½ cup firmly packed light brown sugar

½ cup butter, melted

1 Tbsp. all-purpose flour

1 Tbsp. plain yellow cornmeal

1 Tbsp. apple cider vinegar

1 tsp. vanilla extract

¼ tsp. table salt

4 large eggs

Whipped Cream (p. 256)

Shoofly Pie

MAKES 8 SERVINGS   **HANDS-ON TIME 28 MIN.**   **TOTAL TIME 3 HR., 40 MIN.**

This delightfully gooey pie is layered with a crumbly mixture of sugar and spices. It's not shoofly pie unless you use molasses!

1. Prepare Simply Piecrust as directed, baking in a 9-inch deep-dish pie plate. Reduce oven temperature to 350°.

2. Process flour and next 7 ingredients in a food processor until crumbly.

3. Stir together boiling water and baking soda in a large bowl; let stand 1 minute. Stir together molasses, corn syrup, vanilla, and egg in a medium bowl; stir into baking soda mixture.

4. Sprinkle half of crumb mixture on bottom of prepared crust. Pour molasses mixture over crumb mixture. Sprinkle remaining crumb mixture over filling.

5. Bake at 350° for 40 minutes or until set. Remove from oven to a wire rack, and cool completely (about 1½ hours).

Pie Fact   *This rich pie, originating with the Amish of Pennsylvania, is not for the faint of heart—its strong molasses flavor is what gives it its Southern charm.*

Ingredients

—1—
SIMPLY PIECRUST

p. 12

plus

1 cup all-purpose flour

⅔ cup firmly packed light brown sugar

3 Tbsp. butter

½ tsp. ground cinnamon

⅛ tsp. ground nutmeg

⅛ tsp. ground ginger

⅛ tsp. ground cloves

⅛ tsp. table salt

½ cup boiling water

½ tsp. baking soda

½ cup light molasses

½ cup light corn syrup

1 tsp. vanilla extract

1 large egg, lightly beaten

Fresh Pumpkin Pie

MAKES 8 SERVINGS **HANDS-ON TIME 30 MIN.** **TOTAL TIME 4 HR., 15 MIN.**

Baking a fresh little sugar pumpkin is no trouble, so bake a couple at a time when they're in season.

1. Prepare Rustic Almond Piecrust through step 2 in a 9-inch deep-dish pie plate.

2. Preheat oven to 425°. Whisk together milk and eggs in a large bowl; add Fresh Pumpkin Puree and next 6 ingredients, whisking until well blended and smooth. Pour mixture into prepared crust.

3. Bake at 425° for 15 minutes; reduce oven temperature to 350°, and bake for 50 to 55 minutes or until a knife inserted near center comes out clean, shielding edges with aluminum foil to prevent excessive browning. Remove from oven to a wire rack, and cool completely (about 3 hours). Serve with Whipped Cream.

Fresh Pumpkin Puree

Preheat oven to 350°. Cut *1 sugar pumpkin* (about 3 lb.) into quarters; discard seeds and stringy pulp. Place wedges on an aluminum foil-lined jelly-roll pan; brush pumpkin flesh with *1 tsp. vegetable oil*. Bake at 350° for 1 hour or until fork-tender. Remove from oven, and cool 30 minutes. Scoop out pumpkin pulp into a food processor; process until smooth.

Ingredients

— 1 —
RUSTIC
ALMOND
PIECRUST

p.16

plus

1 (12-oz.) can
evaporated milk

2 large eggs

1⅔ cups Fresh Pumpkin
Puree or 1 (15-oz.)
can pumpkin

1 cup firmly packed
brown sugar

1 tsp. ground cinnamon

½ tsp. table salt

½ tsp. ground ginger

¼ tsp. ground nutmeg

dash of ground cloves

Whipped Cream
(p. 256)

garnish: candied
almonds pieces

Chocolate Fudge Pie
with Praline Crumble

MAKES **8 SERVINGS**   HANDS-ON TIME **33 MIN.**   TOTAL TIME **5 HR., 23 MIN.**

So rich and chocolaty, this pie is our family favorite for Sunday afternoons with a cup of hot coffee.

1. Prepare Deep South Piecrust through step 2 in a 9-inch pie plate.

2. Preheat oven to 350°. Microwave butter and chocolate morsels in a medium glass bowl at HIGH 1 to 2 minutes or until melted and smooth, stirring at 30-second intervals. Stir in sugars. Stir in eggs. Stir in flour, whipping cream, and vanilla until blended. Pour into prepared crust.

3. Bake at 350° for 45 minutes or until puffed and almost set. (Filling will deflate as it cools.) Remove from oven to a wire rack, and cool completely (about 3 hours).

4. Top each slice with Whipped Cream and Praline Crumble.

Praline Crumble
Preheat oven to 350°. Bring *1½ cups firmly packed light brown sugar, ½ cup whipping cream, 2 Tbsp. butter,* and *1 Tbsp. light corn syrup* to a boil in a medium-size heavy saucepan over medium heat, stirring constantly. Boil, stirring occasionally, 6 to 8 minutes or until a candy thermometer registers 236° (soft ball stage). Remove pan from heat. Let sugar mixture stand until candy thermometer registers 150° (15 to 20 minutes). Stir in *1 tsp. vanilla extract* and *1 cup coarsely chopped pecans* using a wooden spoon; stir constantly 1 minute or just until mixture begins to lose its gloss. Spoon into small mounds onto *wax paper;* let stand until firm (about 10 minutes). Cut into small pieces.

Ingredients

**1
DEEP
SOUTH
PIECRUST**
p.12

plus

¾ cup butter

¾ cup semisweet chocolate morsels

¾ cup firmly packed dark brown sugar

⅔ cup granulated sugar

3 large eggs, lightly beaten

2 Tbsp. all-purpose flour

3 Tbsp. whipping cream

1 tsp. vanilla extract

Whipped Cream (*p. 256*)

Praline Crumble

Down South Muscadine Pie

MAKES 6-8 SERVINGS   HANDS-ON TIME 1 HR., 17 MIN.   TOTAL TIME 1 HR., 57 MIN.

In late summer in Alabama, the muscadines are ripe and ready to eat. The beautiful globes of red and gold with a sweet musky flavor make great wine, delicious jelly, and amazing pie!

1. To prepare Filling: wash muscadines. Cut muscadines in half, and remove seeds (being careful not to discard pulp). Place muscadines in a large heavy saucepan. Add ½ cup water; bring to a boil. Partially cover, reduce heat to medium-low, and simmer 35 minutes or until skins are tender, stirring occasionally.

2. Preheat oven to 350°. Stir together sugar and cornstarch in a small bowl; stir into muscadine mixture. Stir in lemon juice and salt. Pour muscadine mixture into a buttered 11- x 7-inch baking dish.

3. To prepare Topping: Cut crusts from bread slices; arrange bread slices over muscadine mixture. Whisk together sugar, butter, vanilla, and egg in a medium bowl; pour over bread, spreading to cover. Bake at 350° for 40 minutes or until golden brown.

Note: We tested with Pepperidge Farmhouse Hearty White Bread.

Virginia Peanut Pie

MAKES 8 SERVINGS   **HANDS-ON TIME 16 MIN.**   **TOTAL TIME 3 HR., 46 MIN.**

You are probably already familiar with Virginia peanuts. They are the type of peanuts grown all over the South and are great roasted, salted, eaten out of hand, or in a pie! In Alabama we have a long history with peanuts—we turned to peanut farming after boll weevils devoured our cotton crop. The peanuts were such a success that we even have a statue to honor the pesky insect!

1. Prepare Deep South Piecrust through step 2 in a 9-inch pie plate.

2. Preheat oven to 350°. Whisk together sugar and next 5 ingredients in a medium bowl; stir in peanuts. Pour into prepared crust.

3. Bake at 350° for 40 to 45 minutes or until set. Remove from oven to a wire rack, and cool completely (about 3 hours). Serve with ice cream, if desired.

Note: We tested with Lyle's Golden Syrup.

Ingredients

— 1 —
DEEP
SOUTH
PIECRUST

p.12

plus

⅓ cup sugar

⅔ cup golden syrup

⅓ cup creamy
peanut butter

⅓ cup butter,
melted

1 tsp. vanilla extract

3 large eggs,
lightly beaten

1½ cups coarsely
chopped salted
Virginia peanuts

vanilla ice cream
(optional)

Maple *and* Black Walnut Pie

MAKES 10-12 SERVINGS HANDS-ON TIME 11 MIN. TOTAL TIME 51 MIN.

Black walnuts have an intense, assertive flavor. Substitute regular walnuts for a milder version, or use a combination of the two.

1. Prepare Simply Piecrust as directed, baking in a 9-inch pie plate. Reduce oven temperature to 375°.

2. Stir together walnuts and next 8 ingredients in a large bowl; pour into prepared crust.

3. Bake at 375° for 40 to 45 minutes or until filling is set, shielding edges with aluminum foil after 20 minutes to prevent excessive browning. Remove from oven to a wire rack, and cool. Serve slightly warm or at room temperature.

Above and beyond *A decorative edge adds a signature touch to your homemade pie. Look on page 33 for instructions on how to make this beautiful leaf-adorned crust and other alternatives.*

Ingredients

1
SIMPLY PIECRUST
p.12

plus

1 cup chopped black walnuts

½ cup maple syrup

½ cup dark corn syrup

⅓ cup granulated sugar

⅓ cup firmly packed dark brown sugar

⅓ cup butter, melted

1 tsp. vanilla extract

½ tsp. table salt

3 large eggs, beaten

Billie's Holiday Pie

MAKES 8 SERVINGS   HANDS-ON TIME 18 MIN.   TOTAL TIME 3 HR., 1 MIN.

Billie is my mother's oldest and dearest friend. I'm so happy she shared this recipe. You'll be thinking of any and every excuse to make it. Be sure to use 100% cane syrup—a must for best results.

1. Prepare Simply Piecrust through step 2 in a 9-inch pie plate.

2. Preheat oven to 350°. Whisk together sugar and next 9 ingredients until blended. Stir in pecans, raisins, and dates. Pour mixture into prepared crust.

3. Bake at 350° on lower oven rack 45 to 48 minutes or until set, shielding edges with aluminum foil to prevent excessive browning. Remove from oven to a wire rack, and cool completely (2 hours).

Ingredients

— 1 —
SIMPLY
PIECRUST

p. 12

plus

1 cup firmly packed
light brown sugar

1 cup cane syrup

¼ cup butter, melted

1 Tbsp. bourbon

1 Tbsp. white vinegar

1 tsp. vanilla extract

½ tsp. ground cinnamon

⅛ tsp. ground nutmeg

⅛ tsp. table salt

3 large eggs

1 cup toasted
pecan pieces

½ cup raisins

½ cup chopped
dried dates

FRESH
Picked

The only problem with fruit pies is deciding what to pick—
peaches, plums, berries, or apples. I have a good friend
who will declare, "Just pick a place and start."
So that's my advice. This crop of pies is ready for harvest.

FRUIT PIES

Summer Berry Pies *63*

Fresh Strawberry Pie *with* Pretzel Crust *64*

Classic Cherry Pie *67*

Cider Apple Pie *68*

Black Skillet Apple Pie *71*

Spiced Pear Pie *72*

Pear *and* Sweet Cheese Phyllo Pie *75*

Mixed Plum Pie *76*

Fresh Peach *and* Apricot Pie *79*

Brown Turkey Fig Pie *80*

Summer Berry Pies

MAKES 8 SERVINGS HANDS-ON TIME 25 MIN. TOTAL TIME 3 HR., 50 MIN.

Summer berries are so juicy and sweet, there are few things better. These little pies are piled high with berries and baked in 4-inch skillets so you can capture every drop of goodness. Bake these pies with a double crust, a lattice, or whatever you prefer.

1. Prepare Simply Piecrusts through step 1. Roll each recipe of dough to ⅛-inch thickness on a lightly floured surface. Cut each recipe of dough into 2 rounds using a 6½-inch round cutter. Fit 1 dough round into each of 4 (4- to 4½-inch) cast-iron skillets or pie pans, allowing edges of dough to extend over sides of pans. Gather scraps from both dough rounds, and roll to ⅛-inch thickness; cut dough into 4 rounds using a 5½-inch round cutter. Chill piecrusts and dough rounds while preparing filling.

2. Preheat oven to 375°. Place raspberries, blueberries, and blackberries in a large bowl. Stir together sugar, cornstarch, zest, and salt; sprinkle over berries. Drizzle with lemon juice, and gently toss to coat.

3. Spoon berry mixture evenly into prepared piecrusts; dot with butter. Place dough rounds on top of filling; press edges of crusts together to seal, and crimp. Cut slits in top for steam to escape. Place pies on an aluminum foil-lined jelly-roll pan.

4. Bake at 375° for 55 minutes or until filling is bubbly and crust is golden brown. Cool completely on a wire rack (about 2 hours).

Ingredients

—2—
SIMPLY
PIECRUSTS

p. 12

plus

1½ cups fresh
raspberries

1½ cups fresh
blueberries

1½ cups fresh
blackberries

¾ cup sugar

¼ cup cornstarch

1 tsp. lemon zest

⅛ tsp. table salt

1 Tbsp. fresh
lemon juice

2 Tbsp. butter,
cut into pieces

Fresh Strawberry Pie *with* Pretzel Crust

MAKES 8 SERVINGS   HANDS-ON TIME 20 MIN.   TOTAL TIME 4 HR., 4 MIN.

Is there anyone who can turn down a piece of fresh strawberry pie? Bright, juicy strawberries suspended in a tart strawberry filling and topped with fresh whipped cream bring back childhood memories of standing at the sink, slicing berries, and sneaking a nibble whenever possible.

1. Prepare Pretzel Piecrust as directed, baking in a 9-inch pie plate.

2. Stir together sugar and cornstarch in a small saucepan; gradually add 1 cup water, whisking until smooth. Bring to a boil, whisking constantly. Boil, whisking constantly, 1 minute or until thickened. Remove from heat; add gelatin, whisking until gelatin dissolves. Cool 15 minutes.

3. Toss together strawberries and gelatin mixture in a large bowl. Spoon into prepared crust. Cover loosely, and chill 3 hours or until set. Serve with Whipped Cream.

Above and beyond To give your pie a fluted crust as pictured, just prepare Pretzel Piecrust in a 9-inch deep-dish fluted tart pan.

Ingredients

— 1 —
PRETZEL
PIECRUST

p. 28

plus

½ cup sugar

2½ Tbsp. cornstarch

½ (3-oz.) package
strawberry gelatin
(3 Tbsp.)

4 cups sliced
fresh strawberries

Whipped Cream
(p. 256)

Classic Cherry Pie

MAKES 8 SERVINGS   **HANDS-ON TIME 25 MIN.**   **TOTAL TIME 4 HR.**

If you love fresh cherry pie, invest in a cherry pitter—it makes fast work of a tedious task. Fresh cherry filling is a labor of love that won't go unrequited.

1. Prepare Simply Piecrusts through step 1.

2. Preheat oven to 375°. Stir together cherries and next 4 ingredients in a large bowl.

3. Roll 1 recipe of Simply Piecrust dough into a 13-inch circle on a lightly floured surface; fit into a 9-inch pie plate. Spoon filling into prepared crust.

4. Roll remaining recipe of Simply Piecrust dough into an 11-inch circle on a lightly floured surface; cut piecrust into 1-inch-wide strips. Arrange strips in a lattice design over filling; gently press ends of strips, sealing to bottom piecrust.

5. Place an aluminum foil-lined jelly-roll pan on lower oven rack. Place pie on middle oven rack over jelly-roll pan to collect juices. Bake at 375° for 1 hour and 5 minutes or until juices are thick and bubbly in center and crust is golden brown, shielding edges with aluminum foil after 45 minutes to prevent excessive browning. Remove from oven to a wire rack, and cool completely (about 2 hours). Serve with ice cream, if desired.

Ingredients

—2—
SIMPLY
PIECRUSTS

p. 12

plus

5 cups fresh or frozen pitted tart red cherries, thawed and drained

1⅓ cups sugar

¼ cup cornstarch

¼ tsp. almond extract

⅛ tsp. table salt

vanilla ice cream (optional)

Cider Apple Pie

MAKES 8 SERVINGS   **HANDS-ON TIME 1 HR., 3 MIN.**   **TOTAL TIME 5 HR., 31 MIN.**

In the fall when apples are plentiful, it's so satisfying to bake an apple pie. If you want to skip the pie plate for your mama's ironstone dish, that gives you more room for Apple Cider Drizzle, and that's always a good thing!

1. Prepare Simply Piecrusts through step 1.

2. Preheat oven to 400°. Combine apples, sugar, flour, ginger, lemon zest, cinnamon, salt, and ½ cup Apple Cider Drizzle in a large bowl; toss gently to coat.

3. Roll 1 recipe of Simply Piecrust dough into a 13-inch circle on a lightly floured surface; fit into a 9-inch pie plate. Spoon apple mixture into prepared crust.

4. Roll remaining recipe of Simply Piecrust dough into an 11-inch circle on a lightly floured surface; cut piecrust into 1-inch-wide strips. Arrange strips in a lattice design over filling; gently press ends of strips, sealing to bottom piecrust. Brush piecrust with cream.

5. Place an aluminum foil-lined jelly-roll pan on lower oven rack. Place pie on middle oven rack over jelly-roll pan to collect juices. Bake at 400° for 50 to 55 minutes or until juices are thick and bubbly and crust is golden brown, shielding edges with aluminum foil to prevent excessive browning. Remove from oven to a wire rack, and cool completely (about 2 hours).

6. Microwave remaining ½ cup Apple Cider Drizzle in a small microwave-safe bowl at HIGH 30 seconds or until warm. Spoon over each serving.

Ingredients

**2
SIMPLY
PIECRUSTS**
p. 12

plus

2½ lb. Pink Lady or
Honeycrisp apples
(6 to 7 apples),
peeled and chopped

½ cup sugar

¼ cup all-purpose flour

2 Tbsp. chopped
crystallized ginger

1 tsp. lemon zest

½ tsp. ground cinnamon

¼ tsp. table salt

Apple Cider Drizzle,
divided
(p. 264)

1 Tbsp. whipping cream

Black Skillet Apple Pie

MAKES 8 SERVINGS   **HANDS-ON TIME 16 MIN.**   **TOTAL TIME 2 HR., 24 MIN.**

This cobbler-like apple pie has thick, luscious juices—perfect for spooning over vanilla ice cream. In the words of the great Southerner Mark Twain, "I know the look of an apple that is roasting and sizzling on the hearth on a winter's evening, and I know the comfort that comes of eating it hot, along with some sugar and a drench of cream."

1. Preheat oven to 375°. Prepare Simply Piecrust through step 1. Roll dough into a 12-inch circle on a lightly floured surface. Place on a baking sheet; cover and chill until ready to use.

2. Stir together granulated sugar and next 5 ingredients. Melt butter in a 10-inch cast-iron skillet over medium-high heat. Add apples; sprinkle with granulated sugar mixture, and toss to coat. Remove from heat.

3. Place chilled dough over apple mixture; brush with egg. Cut 3 slits in top for steam to escape; sprinkle with coarse sugar.

4. Bake at 375° for 40 minutes or until crust is golden brown and apples are tender. Remove from oven to a wire rack, and let stand 20 minutes before serving.

Ingredients

— 1 —
SIMPLY
PIECRUST
p. 12

plus

⅓ cup granulated sugar

⅓ cup firmly packed brown sugar

2 Tbsp. all-purpose flour

½ tsp. apple pie spice

½ tsp. ground cinnamon

⅛ tsp. table salt

2 Tbsp. butter

6 Fuji apples, peeled and cut into ½-inch-thick wedges (3 lb.)

1 large egg, lightly beaten

1 Tbsp. coarse or turbinado sugar

Spiced Pear Pie

MAKES 8 SERVINGS   HANDS-ON TIME 38 MIN.   TOTAL TIME 5 HR., 38 MIN.

I love the delicate flavor of the pears mingled with spices and the rich flavor of the sorghum. Sprinkling the crust with sparkling sugar just before baking makes a pretty presentation and adds a lovely little crunch.

1. Prepare Simply Piecrusts through step 1.

2. Preheat oven to 375°. Roll 1 recipe of Simply Piecrust dough into a 13-inch circle on a floured surface; fit into a 9-inch pie plate.

3. Stir together granulated sugar and next 6 ingredients in a large bowl. Add sliced pears, sorghum syrup, and zest, tossing gently to coat. Spoon pear mixture into prepared crust.

4. Roll remaining recipe of Simply Piecrust dough into an 11-inch circle on a lightly floured surface. Place dough over pear mixture; fold edges under, and crimp. Cut slits in top for steam to escape. Brush piecrust with egg, and sprinkle with sparkling sugar.

5. Place an aluminum foil-lined jelly-roll pan on lower oven rack. Place pie on middle oven rack over jelly-roll pan to collect juices. Bake at 375° for 1 hour or until crust is golden brown, shielding edges with aluminum foil to prevent excessive browning. Remove from oven to a wire rack, and cool completely (about 4 hours).

Ingredients

**— 2 —
SIMPLY
PIECRUSTS**

p. 12

plus

½ cup granulated sugar

⅓ cup all-purpose flour

1 tsp. ground cinnamon

¼ tsp. table salt

¼ tsp. ground ginger

¼ tsp. ground nutmeg

⅛ tsp. ground cardamom

3 lb. firm, ripe Bosc pears (5 medium), peeled and sliced

⅓ cup sorghum syrup

1 tsp. orange zest

1 large egg, lightly beaten

2 tsp. white sparkling sugar

Pear *and* Sweet Cheese Phyllo Pie

MAKES 8 SERVINGS   HANDS-ON TIME 12 MIN.   TOTAL TIME 1 HR., 43 MIN.

This elegant pie combines flavors you're probably used to enjoying in a fancy appetizer. Here we've sweetened the pears with brown sugar and brandy and nestled them in luscious goat cheese and crispy phyllo, making this pie the perfect finish to a dinner party.

1. Prepare Phyllo Piecrust as directed, baking in a 9-inch pie plate.

2. Beat cream cheese, goat cheese, and butter at medium speed with an electric mixer until creamy. Gradually add powdered sugar, beating until fluffy. Gently spread into prepared crust. Chill 1 hour.

3. Whisk together brown sugar, brandy, and cornstarch in a medium saucepan; cook over medium-high heat, stirring often, 2 minutes or until sugar dissolves. Add pears; cook, stirring occasionally, 3 minutes or until pears are tender and mixture is bubbly. Transfer to a bowl; chill 30 minutes.

4. Drain pears, reserving syrup. Spoon pears over cheese mixture in crust; sprinkle with walnuts. Serve pie with reserved syrup from pears.

Tip Take a little liberty when slicing your pears. You can core them and cut them into traditional half-moon slices, or you can cut them horizontally into rounds for a more striking look.

Ingredients

— 1 —
PHYLLO
PIECRUST

p. 31

plus

4 oz. cream cheese,
softened

4 oz. goat cheese,
softened

2 Tbsp. butter,
softened

½ cup powdered sugar

⅓ cup firmly packed
light brown sugar

2 Tbsp. brandy

2 tsp. cornstarch

3 firm, ripe pears,
peeled and thinly sliced

⅓ cup chopped walnuts,
toasted

Mixed Plum Pie

MAKES 6-8 SERVINGS   HANDS-ON TIME 25 MIN.   TOTAL TIME 3 HR., 15 MIN.

Whether you find your plums at the farmers' market, your backyard, or the grocery store, pick the ripest ones for the ultimate pie. I like to mix several varieties of plums for unexpected color and flavors.

1. Prepare Deep South Piecrusts through step 1.

2. Preheat oven to 375°. Roll 1 recipe of dough into a 14-inch circle on a lightly floured surface; fit into a 9½-inch deep-dish pie plate.

3. Toss together plums, lemon juice, and vanilla in a large bowl. Stir together granulated sugar, cornstarch, cinnamon, and salt in a small bowl; sprinkle over plum mixture, and toss to coat. Spoon plum mixture into prepared crust.

4. Roll remaining recipe of dough into a 12-inch circle on a lightly floured surface. Place piecrust on top of plum mixture in pie plate; fold edges under, and crimp. Cut 2 to 4 slits in top for steam to escape. Brush piecrust with egg, and sprinkle with sparkling sugar.

5. Bake at 375° for 45 to 50 minutes or until filling is bubbly and crust is golden brown, shielding edges with aluminum foil to prevent excessive browning. Remove from oven to a wire rack, and cool completely.

Ingredients

— 2 —
DEEP SOUTH
PIECRUSTS

p.12

plus

5 cups (½-inch-thick)
sliced ripe plums
(9 large)

2 Tbsp. fresh
lemon juice

1 tsp. vanilla extract

¾ cup granulated sugar

3 Tbsp. cornstarch

¼ tsp. ground cinnamon

¼ tsp. table salt

1 large egg, beaten

1 Tbsp. sparkling sugar

Fresh Peach *and* Apricot Pie

MAKES 8 SERVINGS   HANDS-ON TIME 30 MIN.   TOTAL TIME 2 HR., 10 MIN.

Peaches and apricots make such a cheery combination; it's like taking a bite out of a sunny day.

1. Prepare Simply Piecrusts through step 1.

2. Preheat oven to 375°. Stir together sugar, cornstarch, and salt in a large bowl; add peach and apricot slices, tossing gently to coat. Add apricot preserves and almond extract; toss gently to coat.

3. Roll 1 recipe of Simply Piecrust dough into a 13-inch circle on a floured surface; fit into a 9-inch pie plate. Spoon fruit mixture into prepared crust.

4. Roll remaining recipe of Simply Piecrust dough into an 11-inch circle on a lightly floured surface. Place dough over fruit mixture; fold edges under, and crimp. Cut 2 to 4 slits in top for steam to escape. Brush piecrust with cream.

5. Bake at 375° for 50 minutes or until juices are thick and bubbly and crust is golden brown. Remove from oven to a wire rack, and cool completely.

Tip Notice the sweet little pie bird in the photo? He is so helpful when making a double-crust pie—he allows the steam to escape from his beak so the pie filling won't seep out the pie edges.

Ingredients

— 2 —
SIMPLY
PIECRUSTS

p. 12

plus

1 cup sugar

¼ cup cornstarch

¼ tsp. table salt

2 cups fresh peach slices

2 cups fresh apricot slices

⅓ cup apricot preserves

⅛ tsp. almond extract

1 Tbsp. whipping cream

Brown Turkey Fig Pie

MAKES 8 SERVINGS   **HANDS-ON TIME 30 MIN.**   **TOTAL TIME 3 HR., 30 MIN.**

You have to be quick around our house to keep enough fresh figs on hand to bake a pie. They disappear quickly if you don't keep a close watch. I like Brown Turkey, but any kind of fresh figs will do for this pie. The Rustic Almond Piecrust is fantastic with these sugared figs, but try any crust you like.

1. Prepare Rustic Almond Piecrusts through step 1.

2. Preheat oven to 375°. Roll 1 recipe of dough into a 13-inch circle on a lightly floured surface; fit into a 9-inch pie plate.

3. Combine brown sugar, cornstarch, and cinnamon in a large bowl. Add figs; toss to coat. Stir together sorghum syrup and next 3 ingredients in a small bowl; drizzle over fig mixture. Spoon fig filling into prepared crust.

4. Roll remaining recipe of dough into an 11-inch circle on a lightly floured surface; cut into 1-inch-wide strips. Arrange strips in a lattice design over filling; gently press ends of strips into bottom piecrust; crimp edge of crust.

5. Bake at 375° for 40 to 45 minutes or until filling is bubbly and crust is golden brown, shielding edges with aluminum foil to prevent excessive browning. Remove from oven to a wire rack, and cool completely.

Ingredients

——2——
RUSTIC
ALMOND
PIECRUSTS

p.16

plus

½ cup firmly packed
light brown sugar

3 Tbsp. cornstarch

¼ tsp. ground cinnamon

16 ripe Brown Turkey
figs, stemmed and cut
into fourths (4 cups)

¼ cup sorghum syrup

2 tsp. orange zest

3 Tbsp. fresh
orange juice

¼ tsp. table salt

WHIPPED

Together

Oh, my. Cream pies, with lofty swirls of whipped cream or a golden billowy meringue, are just about the best way to bring a smile to someone's face. It just doesn't get much better, except sharing a piece with someone you love.

CREAM, MERINGUE & ICE-CREAM PIES

Red Velvet Pie *85*

Banana Cream Pie *86*

Lemon Pie *with* Basil Whipped Cream *89*

Mixed Berry Cream Pie *90*

Margarita Key Lime Pie *with* Coconut Piecrust *93*

Lemon Icebox Pie *94*

Daddy's Triple Coconut Cream Pie *97*

Dark Chocolate Cream Pie *98*

Zebra Pie *101*

Seriously Black Bottom Pie *102*

Jim's Graham Cracker Pie *105*

Sweet Potato Pie *with* Marshmallow Meringue *106*

Butterscotch Pie *109*

Frozen Orange Cream Pie *110*

Frosty Peppermint Pie *113*

Peanut Butter Candy Pie *114*

Mocha Mud Pie *117*

Red Velvet Pie

MAKES 8-10 SERVINGS   HANDS-ON TIME 48 MIN.   TOTAL TIME 6 HR., 48 MIN.

My sister Nancy is famous for her Red Velvet Cake, so I thought it might be fun to try it as a pie. With a butter-milk-chocolate filling and whipped cream cheese topping, this pie tastes just like its namesake. For the cleanest slice, be sure to whip the cream cheese topping until very firm.

1. Prepare Simply Piecrust as directed, baking in a 9-inch pie plate.

2. Meanwhile, whisk together sugar, cornstarch, and cocoa in a medium saucepan. Whisk in cream, buttermilk, and eggs. Bring to a boil over medium heat, whisking constantly. Boil, whisking constantly, 1 minute or until thickened. Remove from heat; stir in food coloring and vanilla.

3. Pour mixture into prepared crust, and cool 1 hour. Cover and chill until set (about 3 hours).

4. Spoon Whipped Cream Cheese Topping over filling, and sprinkle with Glazed Pecans.

Glazed Pecans

Preheat oven to 350°. Line a jelly-roll pan with **parchment paper;** coat parchment paper with cooking spray. Stir together **¼ cup dark corn syrup** and **2 Tbsp. sugar.** Add **2 cups pecan halves;** stir until pecans are coated. Spread pecans in a single layer in prepared pan. Bake at 350° for 15 minutes or until glaze bubbles slowly and thickens, stirring every 3 minutes. Transfer pan to a wire rack. Spread pecans in a single layer, separating individual pecans; cool completely (about 30 minutes). Cooled pecans should be crisp; if not, bake 5 more minutes.

Ingredients

— 1 —
SIMPLY
PIECRUST

p. 12

plus

¾ cup sugar

⅓ cup cornstarch

⅓ cup unsweetened cocoa

2 cups whipping cream

1 cup whole buttermilk

4 large eggs, lightly beaten

1 (1-oz.) bottle red liquid food coloring

2 tsp. vanilla extract

Whipped Cream Cheese Topping *(p. 256)*

Glazed Pecans

Banana Cream Pie

MAKES 8-10 SERVINGS   **HANDS-ON TIME 22 MIN.**   **TOTAL TIME 5 HR., 34 MIN.**

Banana Cream Pie is my go-to comfort food. You might prefer a graham cracker crust or cream cheese pastry, but it's good any way you slice it.

1. Prepare Vanilla Wafer Piecrust as directed, baking in a 9½-inch deep-dish pie plate.

2. Whisk together sugar and cornstarch in a heavy saucepan. Whisk together half-and-half and eggs. Gradually whisk egg mixture into sugar mixture. Bring to a boil over medium heat, whisking constantly. Boil 1 minute; remove from heat. Add butter, vanilla, and salt, stirring until butter melts. Place pan in ice water; whisk custard occasionally until cool.

3. Cut bananas into ¼-inch slices; arrange slices over bottom of cooled crust. Spoon custard over bananas. Place heavy-duty plastic wrap directly on warm custard (to prevent a film from forming); chill 4 hours or until set. (Filling will thicken as it chills.) Top with Whipped Cream.

 Tip Be sure to whip the cream until just stiff before topping the pie so that it will slice beautifully.

Ingredients

— 1 —
VANILLA
WAFER
PIECRUST

p. 24

plus

1 cup sugar

⅓ cup cornstarch

3 cups half-and-half

3 large eggs

5 Tbsp. butter,
cut into pieces

1 tsp. vanilla extract

¼ tsp. table salt

3 large ripe bananas

Whipped Cream
(p. 256)

Lemon Pie *with* Basil Whipped Cream

MAKES 8-10 SERVINGS   **HANDS-ON TIME 32 MIN.**   **TOTAL TIME 5 HR., 37 MIN.**

Basil Whipped Cream is such a lovely complement to this creamy lemon pie. Be sure to use the freshest basil possible.

1. Prepare Simply Piecrust as directed, baking in a 9-inch pie plate.

2. Whisk together sugar, cornstarch, and salt in a medium-size heavy nonaluminum saucepan.

3. Whisk together egg yolks and next 2 ingredients in a medium glass bowl; whisk into sugar mixture in pan. Bring to a boil over medium heat, whisking constantly. Boil, whisking constantly, 1 minute or until thickened. Remove from heat. Stir in butter, zest, and, if desired, food coloring until smooth; pour into prepared crust. Remove from oven to a wire rack, and cool completely (about 1 hour). Cover and chill until set (about 2 hours).

4. Prepare Basil Whipped Cream. Spread over filling; cover loosely, and chill until ready to serve.

Tip *Basil Whipped Cream gives this pie a summery brightness. If you want to try something different, top it with Sweet Mint Whipped Cream or plain Whipped Cream.*

Ingredients

— 1 —
SIMPLY
PIECRUST

p. 12

plus

1½ cups sugar

⅓ cup cornstarch

⅛ tsp. table salt

4 large egg yolks

1¾ cups milk

½ cup fresh lemon juice

3 Tbsp. butter

1 tsp. lemon zest

drop of yellow liquid food coloring (optional)

Basil Whipped Cream (p. 256)

garnish: small basil leaves

Mixed Berry Cream Pie

MAKES 8 SERVINGS   HANDS-ON TIME 15 MIN.   TOTAL TIME 4 HR., 30 MIN.

A perfect pie for celebrating summer: Take fresh berries, bury them in a creamy mascarpone filling and shortbread crust, and drizzle with orange-berry nectar—it doesn't get any yummier than that.

Ingredients

—1—
SHORTBREAD
COOKIE
PIECRUST

p. 24

plus

2 cups fresh
strawberries,
quartered and divided

1½ cups
fresh blueberries,
divided

1 (6-oz.) package
fresh raspberries,
divided

2 Tbsp. granulated
sugar

2 Tbsp. orange liqueur

1 tsp. orange zest

1½ cups heavy cream

¾ cup powdered sugar

1½ (8-oz.) containers
mascarpone cheese

1 tsp. vanilla extract

1. Prepare Shortbread Cookie Piecrust as directed, baking in a 9-inch pie plate.

2. Combine 1 cup strawberries, ¾ cup blueberries, and half of raspberries in a bowl, mashing with a potato masher until chunky. Stir granulated sugar, liqueur, and zest into mashed berries. Cover and let stand 30 minutes; drain well, reserving liquid. Cover and chill remaining berries.

3. Meanwhile, beat cream and next 3 ingredients at high speed with an electric mixer until stiff peaks form.

4. Spoon half of cream mixture into prepared crust. Top with drained mashed berry mixture and remaining half of cream mixture. Cover and chill 3 hours or until firm.

5. Uncover, top with chilled berries, and drizzle with reserved liquid just before serving.

Note: We tested with Grand Marnier.

Margarita Key Lime Pie
with Coconut Piecrust

MAKES 8 SERVINGS   **HANDS-ON TIME 20 MIN.**   **TOTAL TIME 6 HR., 3 MIN.**

I know the number of limes you have to squeeze looks daunting, but trust me, it's worth it to get that bright and powerful pure lime flavor. Don't you dare use a bottled juice—that's cheating!

1. Prepare Coconut Piecrust as directed, baking in a 9-inch pie plate.

2. Preheat oven to 350°. Beat egg yolks and 2 tsp. zest at high speed with a heavy-duty electric stand mixer, using whisk attachment, until thick and pale (about 5 minutes). Reduce speed to medium; gradually add condensed milk in a slow, steady stream, beating constantly. Add lime juice, tequila, and orange liqueur; beat just until blended. Pour filling into prepared crust.

3. Bake at 350° for 13 minutes or until filling is set. Remove from oven to a wire rack, and cool completely (about 40 minutes).

4. Cover and chill at least 4 hours; top with Whipped Cream.

Ingredients

—1—
COCONUT
PIECRUST
p. 19

plus

3 large egg yolks

2 tsp. lime zest

1 (14-oz.) can
sweetened
condensed milk

¾ cup fresh
Key lime juice
(about 22 Key limes)

2 Tbsp. tequila

1 Tbsp. orange liqueur

Whipped Cream
(p. 256)

garnish: Key lime zest,
Key lime slices

Lemon Icebox Pie

MAKES 8 SERVINGS   **HANDS-ON TIME 9 MIN.**   **TOTAL TIME 4 HR., 14 MIN.**

*In the South, this pie is almost as iconic as sweet tea.
It's a must as the final flourish at any barbecue.*

Ingredients

—— 1 ——
GRAHAM
CRACKER
PIECRUST

p. 27

plus

6 large egg yolks

1 tsp. lemon zest

1 cup fresh lemon juice
(7 large lemons)

2 (14-oz.) cans
sweetened
condensed milk

Whipped Cream
(p. 256)

1. Prepare Graham Cracker Piecrust through step 1 in a 9½-inch deep-dish pie plate.

2. Preheat oven to 325°. Beat egg yolks at medium-high speed with an electric mixer until thick and pale (about 5 minutes). Add lemon zest, lemon juice, and condensed milk, beating just until blended.

3. Pour into prepared crust. Bake at 325° for 20 minutes or until crust is browned and filling is almost set. Remove from oven to a wire rack, and cool completely (about 1 hour).

4. Cover and chill at least 2 hours or until set. Top with Whipped Cream.

Tip Don't forget to use a deep-dish pie plate for this recipe—it's an especially generous Lemon Icebox Pie, and it will overflow a regular 9-inch pie plate.

Daddy's Triple Coconut Cream Pie

MAKES 8 SERVINGS   **HANDS-ON TIME 14 MIN.**   **TOTAL TIME 3 HR., 19 MIN.**

My daddy loves coconut. With coconut in the crust, in the custard, and on top, this creamy confection is a coconut lover's dream.

1. Prepare Coconut Piecrust as directed, baking in a 9-inch pie plate.

2. Whisk together sugar and cornstarch in a medium-size heavy saucepan. Whisk together milk and eggs. Gradually whisk milk mixture into sugar mixture; bring to a boil over medium heat, whisking constantly. Boil 1 minute or until thickened, whisking constantly. Remove from heat.

3. Add butter, extract, and salt, stirring until butter melts. Stir in 1½ cups coconut. Pour into baked crust. Place plastic wrap directly onto warm custard (to prevent a film from forming), and cool on a wire rack 30 minutes. Chill 2 hours or until set and thoroughly chilled.

4. Preheat oven to 350°. Place remaining ¼ cup coconut in a single layer in a shallow pan. Bake at 350° for 5 to 6 minutes or until toasted, stirring occasionally.

5. Spread Whipped Cream over pie. Sprinkle with toasted coconut.

Ingredients

—1—
COCONUT
PIECRUST

p.19

plus

1 cup sugar

⅓ cup cornstarch

3 cups milk

4 large eggs

⅓ cup butter

½ tsp. coconut extract

¼ tsp. table salt

1¾ cups sweetened flaked coconut, divided

Whipped Cream (p. 256)

Dark Chocolate Cream Pie

MAKES 8 SERVINGS   **HANDS-ON TIME 14 MIN.**   **TOTAL TIME 3 HR., 57 MIN.**

Dutch process cocoa powder gives the dark color and intense flavor to this radically chocolate cream pie. It has layer upon layer of chocolate goodness.

Ingredients

— 1 —
SANDWICH
COOKIE
PIECRUST

p.23

plus

⅔ cup Dutch process cocoa

⅔ cup boiling water

1 cup sugar

⅓ cup cornstarch

¼ tsp. table salt

2½ cups milk

3 large egg yolks

5 Tbsp. butter

2 tsp. vanilla extract

1 cup semisweet chocolate chunks

Whipped Cream *(p. 256)*

garnish: dark chocolate shavings

1. Prepare Sandwich Cookie Piecrust as directed, using chocolate sandwich cookies and baking in a 9-inch pie plate.

2. Place cocoa in a small bowl. Gradually add boiling water, stirring until smooth; cool.

3. Combine sugar, cornstarch, and salt in a medium saucepan. Whisk together milk and egg yolks until blended. Gradually whisk milk mixture into sugar mixture. Bring to a boil; boil, stirring constantly, 1 minute or until thickened.

4. Remove pan from heat; add cocoa mixture and butter, whisking until butter melts and mixture is smooth. Whisk in vanilla.

5. Sprinkle chocolate chunks over bottom of prepared crust. Pour filling over chocolate chunks. Place heavy-duty plastic wrap directly onto warm filling (to prevent a film from forming); chill at least 3 hours or until cold. (Mixture will thicken as it cools.)

6. Spread Whipped Cream on top of pie before serving.

Zebra Pie

MAKES 8–10 SERVINGS   HANDS-ON TIME 15 MIN.   TOTAL TIME 15 MIN. PLUS 1 DAY FOR CHILLING

Perfect for days when you need a quick but decadent dessert, this no-bake icebox pie is super simple to make. To keep the chocolate wafers from lifting up when you spread the whipped cream, first pipe a layer of whipped cream, and then gently spread it with a spatula.

1. Spoon Whipped Cream into a zip-top plastic freezer bag. Snip 1 corner of bag to make a hole about 1 inch in diameter.

2. Arrange one-third of chocolate wafers in bottom of a 9-inch spring-form pan; pipe one-third of Whipped Cream over wafers, spreading evenly with a spatula. Sprinkle with one-third of semisweet chocolate. Repeat layers twice. Cover and chill 8 to 24 hours.

3. Drizzle with fudge sauce, and sprinkle with toffee candy bars just before serving.

Note: We tested with Nabisco Famous Chocolate Wafers, usually stocked near the ice-cream toppings in supermarkets.

Tip *For an even easier version, use whipped topping in place of whipped cream. You can also serve this dessert frozen for a firmer texture with crunchier cookies.*

Ingredients

Whipped Cream *(p. 256)*

1½ (9-oz.) packages chocolate wafers (60 wafers)

1 (4-oz.) semisweet chocolate baking bar, finely chopped

¼ cup hot fudge sauce, warmed

2 (1.4-oz.) chocolate-covered toffee candy bars, chopped

Seriously Black Bottom Pie

MAKES 8 SERVINGS   **HANDS-ON TIME 1 HR., 12 MIN.**   **TOTAL TIME 5 HR., 27 MIN.**

This pie has evolved each time I make it. For those who can't decide on gingersnaps or graham crackers for a crust, I did half and half. It has big, bold flavor—a seriously dark chocolate bottom and a rockin' rum custard—not for the faint of heart. This is not your mama's black bottom pie.

Ingredients

— 1 —
GINGERSNAP-
GRAHAM
CRACKER
PIECRUST

p. 27

plus

1 envelope
unflavored gelatin

¼ cup dark rum

2 cups milk

⅔ cup granulated sugar

1 Tbsp. cornstarch

4 large egg yolks

1¼ cups semisweet
chocolate morsels,
divided

1 cup plus 2 Tbsp.
whipping cream,
divided

2 Tbsp. powdered sugar

1. Prepare Gingersnap-Graham Cracker Piecrust as directed, baking in a 9½-inch deep-dish pie plate.

2. Sprinkle gelatin over rum in a small bowl; stir and let stand 1 minute.

3. Whisk together milk and next 3 ingredients in a medium-size heavy saucepan. Bring to a boil over medium heat, whisking constantly. Boil, whisking constantly, 1 minute or until thickened. Remove from heat; add gelatin mixture, stirring until gelatin dissolves.

4. Combine 1 cup hot custard mixture and 1 cup chocolate morsels in a medium bowl, stirring until chocolate melts and mixture is smooth. Pour chocolate custard into prepared crust; chill 30 minutes or until set.

5. Meanwhile, beat 1 cup whipping cream at high speed with an electric mixer until foamy; add powdered sugar, beating until stiff peaks form. Fold whipped cream into remaining custard mixture. Spread over chocolate custard in crust.

6. Microwave remaining 2 Tbsp. whipping cream and remaining ¼ cup chocolate morsels in a small microwave-safe bowl at HIGH 30 seconds or until chocolate melts and mixture is smooth; drizzle over pie. Cover and chill 3 hours or until firm.

Jim's Graham Cracker Pie

MAKES 8 SERVINGS   HANDS-ON TIME 22 MIN.   TOTAL TIME 6 HR., 10 MIN.

*This old-timey pie is my friend Jim Watkins' favorite.
He's always so proud to bring it to any church supper or
get-together. Don't let its simplicity fool you—it's delicious
and comforting.*

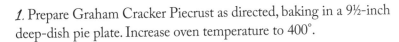

1. Prepare Graham Cracker Piecrust as directed, baking in a 9½-inch
deep-dish pie plate. Increase oven temperature to 400°.

2. Whisk together milk and next 3 ingredients in a heavy saucepan. Bring
to a boil over medium heat, whisking constantly. Boil, whisking constantly,
1 minute or until thickened. Remove pan from heat; add butter, vanilla,
and salt, stirring until butter melts. Pour filling into prepared crust.

3. Spread Mile-High Meringue over warm filling, sealing edges. Sprinkle
meringue with graham cracker crumbs.

4. Bake at 400° for 7 minutes or until meringue is lightly browned.
Remove from oven to a wire rack, and cool completely (about 1 hour).
Cover and chill at least 4 hours.

Above and beyond To make this pie look more elegant,
*try baking the crust in a 9-inch springform pan, pressing crumbs
up sides. Continue with recipe as directed.*

Ingredients

1
GRAHAM
CRACKER
PIECRUST
p. 27

plus

3 cups milk

1 cup sugar

⅓ cup cornstarch

3 large eggs

3 Tbsp. butter

1½ tsp. vanilla extract

¼ tsp. table salt

Mile-High Meringue
(p. 255)

3 Tbsp. graham
cracker crumbs

Sweet Potato Pie *with* Marshmallow Meringue

MAKES 8 SERVINGS   HANDS-ON TIME 30 MIN.   TOTAL TIME 3 HR., 35 MIN.

Sweet Potato Pie is so iconic when you're south of the Mason-Dixon Line. I can't explain the pleasure you feel when you see a big, beautiful slice piled high with marshmallow meringue.

1. Prepare Deep South Piecrust as directed, baking in a 9-inch pie plate. Reduce oven temperature to 350°.

2. Stir together melted butter and next 3 ingredients in a large bowl until well blended. Add sweet potatoes and next 4 ingredients; stir until well blended. Pour sweet potato mixture into prepared crust. (Pie will be very full.)

3. Bake at 350° for 50 to 55 minutes or until a knife inserted in center comes out clean, shielding with aluminum foil to prevent excessive browning. Increase oven temperature to 400°.

4. Spread Marshmallow Meringue over filling. Bake at 400° for 8 to 10 minutes or until meringue is lightly browned.

Ingredients

—1—
DEEP
SOUTH
PIECRUST
p.12

plus

¼ cup butter, melted

1 cup sugar

¼ tsp. table salt

3 large eggs

3 cups lightly packed, mashed cooked sweet potatoes (about 2½ lb. sweet potatoes)

1 cup half-and-half

1 Tbsp. lemon zest

3 Tbsp. lemon juice

¼ tsp. ground nutmeg

Marshmallow Meringue (p. 255)

Butterscotch Pie

MAKES 8 SERVINGS   HANDS-ON TIME 30 MIN.   TOTAL TIME 4 HR.

The Brown Sugar Mile-High Meringue makes this pie a real showstopper.

1. Prepare Simply Piecrust as directed, baking in a 9-inch pie plate. Reduce oven temperature to 325°.

2. Whisk together brown sugar and next 3 ingredients in a large heavy saucepan. Combine egg yolks and milk. Gradually add egg mixture to brown sugar mixture, whisking constantly. Bring mixture to a boil, whisking frequently; cook for 1 minute, whisking constantly, until pudding thickens. Remove from heat; stir in butter and vanilla. Cover and keep warm.

3. Prepare Brown Sugar Mile-High Meringue. Pour butterscotch mixture into prepared crust. Spread meringue over hot filling, sealing edges. Bake at 325° for 25 minutes or until lightly browned. Cool completely on a wire rack (about 2 hours). Store in refrigerator.

Ingredients

— 1 —
SIMPLY
PIECRUST

p. 12

plus

1 cup firmly packed
dark brown sugar

½ cup granulated sugar

⅓ cup cornstarch

⅛ tsp. table salt

3 large egg yolks

2 cups milk

2 Tbsp. butter

1 tsp. vanilla extract

Brown Sugar
Mile-High Meringue
(p. 255)

Frozen Orange Cream Pie

MAKES 8 SERVINGS   HANDS-ON TIME 20 MIN.   TOTAL TIME 5 HR., 12 MIN. PLUS 1 DAY TO MAKE HOMEMADE CRÈME FRAÎCHE

A grown-up version of my favorite creamy orange pop, this pie is so refreshing and satisfying on a hot summer day.

1. Prepare Shortbread Cookie Piecrust as directed, baking in a 9-inch pie plate or in an 8- x 4-inch loaf pan; cool. Place cooled crust in freezer.

2. Beat sorbet and orange juice concentrate at medium speed with an electric mixer until blended. Add Homemade Crème Fraîche and sugar; beat until blended. Pour into crust. Freeze at least 4 hours or until firm.

3. Before serving, top frozen pie with Orange Whipped Cream, and sprinkle with orange zest.

Tip If you are making this pie in a loaf pan, place an 8-inch-wide strip of parchment paper in the pan with the excess hanging over the sides before pressing the crust into the bottom and up the sides of the pan. Use the strips to lift the frozen pie from the pan.

Ingredients

1 SHORTBREAD COOKIE PIECRUST
p. 24

plus

1 pt. orange sorbet, softened

⅓ cup thawed, frozen orange juice concentrate

1 cup Homemade Crème Fraîche *(p. 259)*

1 Tbsp. sugar

½ recipe Orange Whipped Cream *(p. 256)*

1 Tbsp. orange zest

Frosty Peppermint Pie

MAKES 8 SERVINGS   HANDS-ON TIME 20 MIN.   TOTAL TIME 11 HR.

Peppermint ice cream is my absolute favorite. Spooned into a chocolate crust and topped with toasted Italian meringue, it becomes extraordinary. This is my sassy version of Baked Alaska. If you ever needed a reason to buy a kitchen torch, meringues are it—no more hovering around the oven waiting for just the right moment. Just wave the handy wand over the meringue to brown it.

1. Prepare Sandwich Cookie Piecrust as directed, baking in a 9-inch pie plate; cool. Place cooled crust in freezer.

2. Stir ½ cup crushed candies into softened ice cream. Spoon ice-cream mixture into prepared crust. Cover and freeze 8 hours or until firm.

3. Cook granulated sugar, corn syrup, and ¼ cup water in a heavy sauce-pan over medium heat, stirring constantly, until sugar dissolves. Bring to a boil, and boil until a candy thermometer registers 248° (about 4 minutes).

4. Beat egg whites at high speed with an electric mixer until foamy; add salt, and beat until stiff peaks form. Gradually whisk hot syrup into egg whites, whisking until stiff peaks form. Stir in peppermint extract. Spread meringue over pie, sealing edges. Freeze 2 hours or until firm.

5. Preheat broiler. Sprinkle meringue with sparkling sugar. Broil 3 inches from heat 30 seconds or until lightly toasted.

Ingredients

—1—
SANDWICH
COOKIE
PIECRUST
p. 23

plus

½ cup crushed soft
peppermint candies

4 cups peppermint
ice cream,
softened

¾ cup granulated sugar

¼ cup light corn syrup

4 large egg whites

⅛ tsp. table salt

¼ tsp. peppermint
extract

1 tsp. white
sparkling sugar

garnish: crushed soft
peppermint candies

Peanut Butter Candy Pie

MAKES **8 SERVINGS**   HANDS-ON TIME **23 MIN.**   TOTAL TIME **4 HR., 8 MIN.**

This is my daughter Katie's favorite pie. She prefers it to birthday cake on her special day.

1. Prepare Peanut-Graham Cracker Piecrust as directed, baking in a 9-inch pie plate.

2. Beat cream cheese and ½ cup peanut butter at medium speed with an electric mixer until smooth. Gradually add powdered sugar, beating at low speed until blended. Fold in whipped topping. Set aside ¼ cup candies; fold remaining candies into filling. Spoon filling into prepared crust. Chill at least 3 hours.

3. Place remaining 2 Tbsp. peanut butter in a small microwave-safe bowl. Microwave at HIGH 10 seconds; stir. Microwave 10 more seconds; stir until smooth. Drizzle melted peanut butter over pie, and sprinkle with reserved ¼ cup chopped candies.

Ingredients

1
PEANUT-
GRAHAM
CRACKER
PIECRUST

p. 27

plus

1 (8-oz.) package cream cheese, softened

½ cup plus 2 Tbsp. creamy peanut butter, divided

1 cup powdered sugar

2 cups frozen whipped topping, thawed

1 (8-oz.) package miniature peanut butter cup candies, chopped and divided

Mocha Mud Pie

MAKES 8 SERVINGS **HANDS-ON TIME 15 MIN.** **TOTAL TIME 10 HR., 50 MIN.**

A quick glimpse at the ingredient list and you'll know why you should make this pie. It's insanely delicious! The hardest part is waiting for it to freeze.

1. Prepare Sandwich Cookie Piecrust as directed, using chocolate sandwich cookies and baking in a 9-inch pie plate.

2. Fold crumbled cookies and ¾ cup toffee morsels into chocolate ice cream. Gently spread mixture into prepared crust. Cover and freeze 2 hours or until firm.

3. Uncover and spread coffee ice cream over chocolate ice-cream mixture. Cover and freeze overnight.

4. Drizzle Chocolate Ganache over top of pie, and sprinkle with chocolate-covered espresso beans and remaining ¼ cup toffee morsels.

Above and beyond Who says you have to cut a pie into wedges? Slide this frozen pie out of the pie plate, and cut it however you like.

Ingredients

— 1 —
SANDWICH
COOKIE
PIECRUST

p. 23

plus

1 cup crumbled cream-filled chocolate sandwich cookies (about 8 cookies)

1 cup chocolate-covered toffee candy morsels, divided

2 cups chocolate ice cream, softened

2 cups coffee ice cream, softened

Chocolate Ganache (p. 263)

¼ cup chocolate-covered espresso beans, chopped

Rustic to ELEGANT

Whatever your style or occasion, these tarts and galettes are equally impressive, not to mention divinely delicious.

TARTS & GALETTES

Grilled Plum *with* Port Crostata

MAKES 8 SERVINGS   HANDS-ON TIME 24 MIN.   TOTAL TIME 3 HR., 48 MIN.

Grilled plums wrapped in tender cream cheese pastry are fabulous alone, but add a drizzle of the sweet port wine glaze, and they become scandalously good.

1. Prepare Cream Cheese Piecrust through step 2.

2. Combine ruby port, ⅔ cup sugar, and vinegar in a medium saucepan. Bring to a boil over medium-high heat; cook 25 minutes or until syrupy and reduced to 1 cup. Remove from heat, and cool completely (about 30 minutes).

3. Coat cold cooking grate of grill with cooking spray, and place on grill. Preheat grill to 350° to 400° (medium-high) heat. Brush plums with oil; sprinkle cut sides of plums with cinnamon and 2 Tbsp. sugar. Place plums on cooking grate. Grill plums, covered with grill lid, 4 minutes on each side or until tender. Remove plums from grill; cool completely (about 30 minutes). Cut plum halves in half. Preheat oven to 400°. Toss grilled plums with 3 Tbsp. port wine syrup.

4. Roll dough into a 12-inch circle on a lightly floured surface. Fold dough in half, and transfer to a foil-lined baking sheet; unfold dough. Mound plum filling in center of crust, leaving a 2-inch border. Fold dough over plum mixture; fold up sides, and dot with butter. Sprinkle with remaining 1 Tbsp. sugar.

5. Bake at 400° for 45 minutes or until golden. Remove from oven to a wire rack. Drizzle desired amount of remaining port syrup over filling.

Ingredients

1 CREAM CHEESE PIECRUST
p.15

plus

1¾ cups ruby port

⅔ cup sugar

2 Tbsp. red wine vinegar

10 plums, halved and pitted

1½ Tbsp. canola oil

¼ tsp. ground cinnamon

3 Tbsp. sugar, divided

2 Tbsp. butter, cubed

Rosemary Apple Tart

MAKES **10 SERVINGS**   HANDS-ON TIME **24 MIN.**   TOTAL TIME **4 HR., 36 MIN.**

The subtle hint of rosemary is unexpected in this gorgeous tart, accenting the flavor of the tart apples.

Ingredients

— 1 —
LEMON
CORNMEAL
PIECRUST

p.19

plus

6 medium Granny Smith apples, peeled and thinly sliced

2 tsp. lemon zest

2 Tbsp. fresh lemon juice

1 tsp. chopped fresh rosemary

¼ tsp. table salt

⅔ cup plus 1 Tbsp. sugar

3 Tbsp. cold butter, cut into pieces

garnish: fresh rosemary sprigs

1. Prepare Lemon Cornmeal Piecrust through step 1.

2. Preheat oven to 400°. Roll dough to ¼-inch thickness on a lightly floured surface. Fit piecrust into a 10-inch tart pan with removable bottom; press into fluted edges. Fold any excess dough over outside of pan, and pinch to secure to pan. (This will keep piecrust from sliding down pan as it bakes.) Freeze 10 minutes or until firm.

3. Toss together apples, next 4 ingredients, and ⅔ cup sugar in a large bowl. Arrange apple slices, overlapping, in concentric circles in prepared crust. Sprinkle apples with remaining 1 Tbsp. sugar, and dot with butter.

4. Bake at 400° for 50 minutes or until crust is golden brown, shielding edges with aluminum foil after 35 minutes to prevent excessive browning. Remove from oven to a wire rack, and cool completely (about 2 hours).

Tip *By slicing the apples thinly, you are not only ensured a beautiful tart, but also the apples will cook more evenly.*

Cranberry-Orange-Walnut Galette

MAKES 8 SERVINGS   HANDS-ON TIME 20 MIN.   TOTAL TIME 2 HR., 44 MIN.

*All the best flavors of the holidays are baked together
in this charmingly rustic pie.*

1. Prepare Cream Cheese Piecrust through step 2.

2. Preheat oven to 375°. Stir together orange zest, next 5 ingredients,
and 1 cup sugar in a medium saucepan. Bring to a boil over medium-high
heat; reduce heat, and simmer, stirring occasionally, 9 minutes or until
thickened. Remove from heat; cool 20 minutes. Stir in ½ cup walnuts.

3. Roll dough into a 12-inch circle or a 16-inch-long oval on a sheet
of parchment paper. Pour cranberry filling into center of dough, leaving
a 2-inch border. Fold edges of dough over fruit, allowing dough to pleat
as you go. Brush egg white over edges of dough; sprinkle with remaining
1 tsp. sugar. Transfer galette and parchment to a baking sheet.

4. Bake at 375° for 25 minutes or until crust is lightly browned, shielding
edges with aluminum foil to prevent excessive browning. Remove from
oven to a wire rack, and cool completely (about 45 minutes). Serve with
Orange Whipped Cream, if desired.

Ingredients

— 1 —
**CREAM
CHEESE
PIECRUST**
p. 15

plus

1½ tsp. orange zest

¼ cup orange juice

2 Tbsp. orange
marmalade

⅛ tsp. table salt

⅛ tsp. ground cinnamon

1 (12-oz.) package
fresh cranberries

1 cup plus 1 tsp. sugar,
divided

½ cup chopped
toasted walnuts

parchment paper

1 large egg white,
beaten

Orange Whipped
Cream (optional)
(p. 256)

garnish: chopped
toasted walnuts

Apricot Tarte Tatin

MAKES 8 SERVINGS   HANDS-ON TIME 21 MIN.   TOTAL TIME 1 HR., 30 MIN.

I adore a tatin. Think upside-down cake, but made with fresh golden apricots and buttery piecrust. It is as delectable as it is beautiful. You will need your best cast-iron skillet for this.

1. Prepare Simply Piecrust through step 1. Roll dough into a 12-inch circle on a lightly floured work surface; keep chilled.

2. Preheat oven to 400°. Combine sugar and ½ cup water in a 10-inch cast-iron skillet. Cook over medium-high heat 9 minutes or until amber, stirring just until sugar dissolves. Remove from heat; stir in butter, and swirl to coat bottom of pan.

3. Beginning at outside edge, arrange apricot halves, cut sides up, in a circular pattern in syrup, placing 1 apricot half in center of skillet. Sprinkle cardamom over apricot halves. Fit dough over apricot mixture, tucking dough between apricots and edge of skillet.

4. Bake at 400° for 20 minutes or until lightly browned. Remove from oven to a wire rack, and cool 10 minutes. Invert tart onto a serving plate. Serve warm with Homemade Crème Fraîche.

Ingredients

— 1 —
SIMPLY
PIECRUST

p. 12

plus

¾ cup sugar

5 Tbsp. butter

8 fresh apricots, halved
(1¾ lb.)

⅛ tsp. ground
cardamom

Homemade
Crème Fraîche
(p. 259)

Brown Sugar *and* Date Tart

MAKES 10-12 SERVINGS HANDS-ON TIME 15 MIN. TOTAL TIME 4 HR., 14 MIN.

Medjool dates are a wonderfully sweet creamy date. They're a treat by themselves, but when baked in a tart, they turn into a rich, caramel-like filling.

1. Prepare Sweet Pastry through step 2 in a 10-inch tart pan with removable bottom. Preheat oven to 400°. Bake prepared crust for 10 to 12 minutes or just until cooked through. Reduce oven temperature to 350°.

2. Beat brown sugar and next 7 ingredients at medium speed with an electric mixer until blended. Sprinkle dates in prepared crust; pour egg mixture over dates.

3. Bake at 350° for 40 minutes or until set. Remove from oven to a wire rack, and cool completely (about 2 hours). Serve with Bourbon Whipped Cream.

Ingredients

— 1 —
SWEET
PASTRY

p. 20

plus

1 cup firmly packed brown sugar

½ cup sour cream

3 Tbsp. butter, melted

2 tsp. orange zest

1 tsp. vanilla extract

¼ tsp. table salt

¼ tsp. ground cinnamon

3 large eggs

2 cups chopped Medjool dates

Bourbon Whipped Cream *(p. 256)*

garnish: honey, orange zest, and quartered dates

Blackberry-Buttermilk Tart

MAKES 6 SERVINGS HANDS-ON TIME 15 MIN. TOTAL TIME 3 HR., 49 MIN.

Sweet buttermilk and fresh blackberries are the perfect pair in this cool summertime tart.

Ingredients

— 1 —
SHORTBREAD
COOKIE
PIECRUST

p. 24

plus

⅓ cup seedless
blackberry jam

6 Tbsp. sugar

2 Tbsp. cornstarch

⅛ tsp. table salt

1½ cups buttermilk

2 large egg yolks

2 Tbsp. butter

½ tsp. vanilla extract

1 pt. fresh blackberries

garnish: mint leaves

1. Prepare Shortbread Cookie Piecrust through step 1. Preheat oven to 350°. Press Shortbread Cookie Piecrust on bottom and up sides of a 15- x 6-inch tart pan with removable bottom. Bake at 350° for 10 to 12 minutes or until golden brown. Cool completely on a wire rack (about 20 minutes).

2. Spread jam over bottom of cooled crust. Whisk together sugar, cornstarch, and salt in a medium saucepan; whisk in buttermilk and egg yolks. Bring to a boil over medium heat, stirring constantly. Boil, whisking constantly, 1 minute or until thickened. Remove from heat; stir in butter and vanilla.

3. Pour custard into crust. Place heavy-duty plastic wrap directly on warm custard (to prevent a film from forming); chill 3 hours or until set. (Mixture will thicken as it cools.) Top with fresh blackberries before serving.

Tip *For a sweet twist on this tart, substitute seedless raspberry jam and fresh raspberries for the blackberry jam and fresh blackberries.*

Meyer Lemon Tart

MAKES 8-10 SERVINGS HANDS-ON TIME 5 MIN. TOTAL TIME 4 HR., 37 MIN.

If you love lemon bars, then you will love this tart. It's super fast and easy but looks like you spent hours squeezing lemons. It's best with Meyer lemons, but any thin-skinned lemon will work.

1. Prepare Sweet Pastry as directed, baking in a 10-inch tart pan with removable bottom. Reduce oven temperature to 350°.

2. Trim ends from lemon, and cut into 4 wedges; cut each wedge in half crosswise. Remove and discard seeds.

3. Process lemon pieces and next 6 ingredients in a blender until smooth, stopping to scrape down sides as needed. Pour into prepared crust.

4. Bake at 350° for 35 to 40 minutes or until filling is almost set. (Filling will set as it cools.) Remove from oven to a wire rack, and cool completely (about 3 hours). Dust with powdered sugar before serving.

Ingredients

— 1 —
SWEET
PASTRY

p. 20

plus

1 medium-size
Meyer or other
thin-skinned lemon

1¾ cups granulated
sugar

⅓ cup butter,
melted

2 Tbsp. all-purpose
flour

3 Tbsp. whipping cream

⅛ tsp. table salt

4 large eggs

powdered sugar

Fresh Orange Tart *with* Honey-Glazed Pistachios

MAKES 10 SERVINGS   HANDS-ON TIME 24 MIN.   TOTAL TIME 3 HR., 28 MIN.

A feast for the eyes and the palate, fresh oranges and honey arranged over cool creamy yogurt are gorgeous and so refreshing.

1. Prepare Sweet Pastry as directed, baking in a 10-inch round or an 8-inch square tart pan with removable bottom.

2. Stir together cream cheese, sugar, and orange zest in a medium bowl until well blended; stir in yogurt. Spread into prepared crust. Cover and chill at least 1 hour. Prepare Honey-Glazed Pistachios.

3. Using a sharp, thin-bladed knife, cut a ¼-inch-thick slice from both ends of each orange. Place oranges flat ends down on a cutting board, and remove peel in strips, cutting from top to bottom following the curvature of fruit. Remove any remaining bitter white pith. Holding peeled orange in the palm of your hand, slice between membranes, and gently remove whole segments. Discard membranes.

4. Arrange orange sections decoratively over tart just before serving. Sprinkle with Honey-Glazed Pistachios, and drizzle with orange blossom honey.

Honey-Glazed Pistachios

Preheat oven to 350°. Stir together *1 cup pistachios* and *2 tsp. orange blossom honey* in a small bowl. Sprinkle with *1 Tbsp. light brown sugar*, tossing to coat. Spread onto a lightly greased aluminum foil-lined baking sheet. Bake at 350° for 7 minutes. Remove from oven to a wire rack, and cool 30 minutes.

Ingredients

— 1 —
SWEET
PASTRY

p. 20

plus

4 oz. cream cheese, softened

½ cup sugar

1 tsp. orange zest

2 cups plain Greek yogurt

Honey-Glazed Pistachios

3 large navel oranges

2 medium blood oranges

1 Tbsp. orange blossom honey

Caramel-Banana-Walnut Tart

MAKES 9 SERVINGS **HANDS-ON TIME 43 MIN.** **TOTAL TIME 2 HR., 31 MIN.**
PLUS 1 DAY FOR CHILLING

1. Prepare Simply Piecrust as directed, baking in a 9-inch square tart pan
with removable bottom.

2. Stir together ¼ cup water and 1 cup sugar in a medium-size heavy
saucepan. Cook, without stirring, over medium heat 8 minutes or until
sugar begins to caramelize and turn amber in color. Tilt pan to evenly
blend color. Add 3 Tbsp. cream and 2 Tbsp. butter, stirring until caramel
melts and mixture is smooth. Remove from heat, and cool 2 minutes.
Spread caramel in bottom of prepared crust.

3. Whisk together cornstarch and remaining ½ cup sugar in a medium
saucepan. Whisk in egg yolks and remaining 2 cups cream. Bring to a boil
over medium heat; boil 1 minute. Remove from heat; add vanilla, salt,
nutmeg, and remaining 3 Tbsp. butter, stirring until butter melts. Remove
from heat, and cool 5 minutes.

4. Slice 2 bananas; layer slices over caramel. Stir custard; pour over bananas.
Place heavy-duty plastic wrap directly on warm custard; chill overnight.

5. Remove and discard plastic wrap. Slice remaining banana; arrange
slices over custard, and top with Candied Walnuts.

Candied Walnuts

Melt *2 Tbsp. butter* in a medium skillet. Add *½ cup firmly packed light
brown sugar* and *¼ tsp. ground cinnamon;* cook over medium heat, stirring
until sugar dissolves. Add *2 cups coarsely chopped walnuts* and *¼ tsp. table
salt;* cook, stirring constantly, 5 minutes or until toasted and evenly coated.
Remove from heat. Spread nut mixture on a lightly greased baking sheet;
break walnuts apart with a fork while warm. Cool completely.

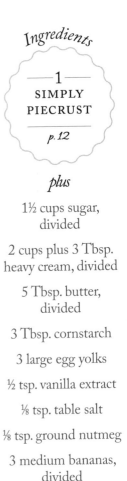

Ingredients

— 1 —
SIMPLY
PIECRUST

p. 12

plus

1½ cups sugar,
divided

2 cups plus 3 Tbsp.
heavy cream, divided

5 Tbsp. butter,
divided

3 Tbsp. cornstarch

3 large egg yolks

½ tsp. vanilla extract

⅛ tsp. table salt

⅛ tsp. ground nutmeg

3 medium bananas,
divided

1 cup Candied Walnuts

Tuxedo Tart

MAKES 12–16 SERVINGS   HANDS-ON TIME 15 MIN.   TOTAL TIME 4 HR., 40 MIN.

This stylish tart is the perfect dinner companion—
a handsome balance of dark and white chocolate.

1. Prepare Chocolate Pastry as directed, baking in a 10-inch tart pan with removable bottom.

2. Microwave dark chocolate morsels, 1 Tbsp. butter, and ½ cup whipping cream in a medium glass bowl at HIGH 1½ minutes or until melted and smooth, stirring at 30-second intervals. Pour over prepared crust, spreading to edges. Chill 30 minutes or until set.

3. Microwave white chocolate and remaining ¼ cup whipping cream in a small glass bowl at HIGH 1 minute or until melted and smooth, stirring at 30-second intervals. Cool completely (about 1 hour), stirring occasionally.

4. Beat white chocolate mixture and remaining 1 cup softened butter at high speed with an electric mixer until well blended. Gradually add powdered sugar, beating until creamy. Spread white chocolate mixture over dark chocolate layer in crust. Chill 1 hour or until firm.

Above and beyond To really push this tart over the top, spike the dark chocolate layer with 1 tsp. of bourbon or raspberry liqueur. Just stir it into the dark chocolate mixture until smooth before spreading into prepared crust.

Ingredients

— 1 —
CHOCOLATE
PASTRY
p. 23

plus

2 cups dark chocolate morsels

1 cup plus 1 Tbsp. butter, softened and divided

¾ cup whipping cream, divided

1½ (4-oz.) white chocolate baking bars, chopped

1½ cups powdered sugar

garnish: dark chocolate curls

Bridge Club Tart

MAKES 8 SERVINGS   HANDS-ON TIME 13 MIN.   TOTAL TIME 3 HR.

My mother has played bridge for almost 50 years. It was always such fun to see the special delicacies she would make when it was her turn to host. It was all about the presentation. This tart is so beautiful, and it doesn't take hours, so you have time to brush up on your bidding skills.

1. Prepare Sweet Pastry through step 1.

2. Preheat oven to 400°. Cut dough log into ¼-inch-thick slices; arrange slices in a single layer over bottom and up sides of a 14- x 5-inch tart pan, trimming edges. Press edges of slices together. Prick dough generously with a fork.

3. Bake at 400° for 17 minutes or until lightly browned. Remove from oven to a wire rack, and cool completely (about 20 minutes).

4. Beat cream cheese at medium speed with an electric mixer until fluffy. Fold in lemon curd. Spread cream cheese mixture in bottom of cooled crust. Chill 1 hour.

5. Cool melted jelly until slightly thickened; spread all but 2 Tbsp. jelly over cream cheese filling. Arrange fresh fruit over tart. Brush fruit with reserved 2 Tbsp. jelly. Cover and chill until ready to serve.

Ingredients

— 1 —
SWEET PASTRY
p. 20

plus

1 (8-oz.) package cream cheese, softened

1 (10-oz.) jar lemon curd

1 (12-oz.) jar red currant jelly, melted

1 cup fresh cherries, pitted

1 cup halved small strawberries

1 cup blackberries

garnish: mini pansies and lemon zest

Fresh Fig *and* Goat Cheese Tart

MAKES 6-8 SERVINGS   HANDS-ON TIME 24 MIN.   TOTAL TIME 2 HR., 10 MIN.

Impress your friends with this unusual, not-so-sweet dessert using figs when they're at their peak.

1. Prepare Sweet Pastry as directed, baking in a 9-inch tart pan with removable bottom.

2. Beat cream cheese and next 4 ingredients at low speed with an electric mixer just until blended. Spread cheese mixture evenly over bottom of prepared crust.

3. Toss together figs, honey, rosemary, and lemon juice. Arrange figs over cheese mixture, and drizzle with any remaining honey mixture. Sprinkle with walnuts. Chill until ready to serve.

Tip In the South, fresh figs are available in late summer and early fall. When you find perfectly ripe figs, cook or eat them as soon as possible because they won't keep for long!

Ingredients

— 1 —
SWEET
PASTRY

p. 20

plus

1 (8-oz.) package cream cheese, softened

⅓ cup powdered sugar

⅓ cup goat cheese

¼ cup sour cream

2 tsp. lemon zest

¾ lb. small fresh figs, stemmed and halved

2 Tbsp. honey

1 tsp. finely chopped fresh rosemary

1 tsp. lemon juice

¼ cup chopped toasted walnuts

garnish: fresh rosemary sprigs

Sweetheart Tart

MAKES 6-8 SERVINGS   **HANDS-ON TIME 16 MIN.**   **TOTAL TIME 2 HR., 32 MIN.**

This is a great tart to serve on Valentine's Day or for a romantic dinner. I love to serve it with a tiny glass of Grand Marnier.

1. Prepare Sweet Pastry as directed, baking in a 10-inch heart-shaped tart pan with removable bottom.

2. Bring ½ cup cream to a simmer in a 1-qt. saucepan over low heat. Place chocolate in a medium bowl. Stir hot cream into chocolate until smooth. Cool 30 minutes or until room temperature, stirring occasionally.

3. Gradually add vanilla bean paste and remaining 1 cup cream to cooled chocolate mixture, beating at medium speed with an electric mixer 2 minutes or until stiff peaks form. Spoon chocolate mixture into prepared crust, spreading to edges.

4. Cut each strawberry in half vertically. Carve a small "V" in center of top of each half, creating a heart-shaped half. Arrange strawberries decoratively over tart.

Ingredients

— 1 —
SWEET PASTRY
p. 20

plus

1½ cups heavy cream, divided

6 oz. white chocolate, finely chopped

1 tsp. vanilla bean paste

15 large strawberries

garnish: white chocolate curls

Caramelized Fresh Fig Tartlets

MAKES 12 TARTLETS   HANDS-ON TIME 1 HR., 7 MIN.   TOTAL TIME 2 HR. PLUS 1 DAY FOR CHILLING

We're always looking for ways to serve fresh figs at our house. We don't mind simply eating them without any fanfare, but these little tartlets will have you fighting over who gets seconds. Make the piecrust and custard a day ahead, and whip these up in a snap.

1. Prepare Cream Cheese Piecrust through step 2.

2. Preheat oven to 350°. Roll dough to ⅛-inch thickness on a floured surface. Cut into 12 rounds using a 3½-inch round cutter, rerolling as needed. Press rounds into a (12-cup) muffin pan, forming cups.

3. Bake at 350° for 17 minutes or until edges are golden brown. Remove from pan to a wire rack, and cool 15 minutes before filling.

4. Melt honey and butter in a large skillet over medium-high heat. Place figs, cut sides down, in skillet; cook 5 minutes or until figs are browned and caramelized, shaking skillet often. Transfer figs to a bowl. Add Madeira to skillet, and cook 1 minute, stirring to loosen particles from bottom of skillet. Remove from heat, and cool 10 minutes.

5. Spoon Alabama Custard Cream evenly into prepared tartlet shells. Arrange figs, cut sides up, over custard; drizzle with 1 Tbsp. Madeira mixture.

Ingredients

1
CREAM
CHEESE
PIECRUST
p. 15

plus

¼ cup honey

2 Tbsp. butter

12 fresh figs, stemmed and cut in half

1 Tbsp. Madeira

Alabama
Custard Cream
(p. 267)

Pineapple Meringue Tartlets

MAKES 8 TARTLETS **HANDS-ON TIME 34 MIN.** **TOTAL TIME 3 HR., 42 MIN.**

Fresh, diced pineapple is crucial for this tartlet. It has a sunny fresh flavor that can't be matched.

1. Preheat oven to 350°. Prepare Graham Cracker Piecrusts through step 1, pressing crumb mixture into 8 (4-inch) pie pans. Bake at 350° for 8 minutes or until lightly browned. Remove from oven to a wire rack, and cool completely (about 20 minutes). Increase oven temperature to 400°.

2. Whisk together sugar, cornstarch, and salt in a medium saucepan. Gradually whisk in pineapple juice and egg yolks. Stir in pineapple. Bring to a boil over medium heat, whisking constantly. Boil, whisking constantly, 1 minute or until thickened. Remove pan from heat; add butter, stirring until butter melts. Cover and keep warm.

3. Prepare Marshmallow Meringue through step 2.

4. Spoon filling into prepared crusts. Spoon Marshmallow Meringue onto warm filling. Bake at 400° for 7 to 8 minutes or until lightly browned. Remove from oven to wire racks, and cool 1 hour. Chill tartlets 2 hours or until set.

5. Loosen edges of tartlets from pans. Carefully remove tartlets from pans. Serve immediately.

Ingredients

— 2 —
GRAHAM CRACKER PIECRUSTS
p. 27

plus

¾ cup sugar

¼ cup cornstarch

⅛ tsp. table salt

1½ cups pineapple juice

3 large egg yolks

2 cups diced fresh pineapple

¼ cup butter, cut up

Marshmallow Meringue *(p. 255)*

Raspberry Phyllo Tartlets

**MAKES 30 TARTLETS   HANDS-ON TIME 9 MIN.   TOTAL TIME 15 MIN.
PLUS 1 DAY FOR HOMEMADE CRÈME FRAÎCHE**

*Good things come in small packages. These tartlets are great
for showers, afternoon tea, or if you just need a quick dessert;
they only take about 15 minutes to prepare.*

Ingredients

2 (1.9-oz.) packages
frozen mini-phyllo
pastry shells

½ cup seedless
raspberry jam

1½ Tbsp. black
raspberry liqueur

Homemade
Crème Fraîche,
chilled *(p. 259)*

3 Tbsp. powdered sugar

30 fresh raspberries
(about 1 cup)

powdered sugar
(optional)

1. Preheat oven to 350°. Place phyllo shells on a baking sheet. Bake at 350°
for 5 minutes or until crisp and golden. Cool.

2. Whisk together jam and liqueur in a small bowl until smooth. Place
Homemade Crème Fraîche and 3 Tbsp. powdered sugar in a small bowl;
whisk until soft peaks form. Drop small dollops of raspberry mixture over
crème fraîche.

3. Divide filling among phyllo shells, swirling mixture slightly with
a spoon just before filling each shell to maintain a marbled appearance.
Top each tartlet with 1 raspberry. Dust tartlets with powdered sugar,
if desired. Serve immediately.

Note: We used Chambord for black raspberry liqueur.

*Tip Be sure to make the crème fraîche from scratch. It's surprisingly
easy, and the store-bought version won't whip up as nicely.*

Chocolate Truffle Tarts *with* Bourbon Whipped Cream

MAKES 6 TARTS   HANDS-ON TIME 13 MIN.   TOTAL TIME 3 HR., 18 MIN.

This radically chocolate tart is guaranteed to satisfy chocolate fanatics. I like mine with an extra large spoonful of Bourbon Whipped Cream.

1. Prepare Chocolate Pastry through step 1.

2. Preheat oven to 400°. Place dough on a lightly floured surface; roll to ⅛-inch thickness. Cut dough into 6 (5-inch) circles. Fit circles into 6 (4-inch, ¾-inch-deep) tartlet pans with fluted edges. Fold excess dough under, and press firmly into fluted edges to secure to pan. (This will keep piecrust from sliding down pan as it bakes.) Prick bottom and sides of piecrust with a fork. Freeze 10 minutes or until firm.

3. Bake at 400° for 12 minutes or until set. Cool completely on a wire rack (about 30 minutes).

4. Place chopped dark chocolate, semisweet chocolate, and butter in a medium glass bowl. Bring cream to a simmer in a medium saucepan over medium heat. Remove from heat. Pour hot cream over chocolates and butter, stirring until melted and smooth. Stir in vanilla.

5. Pour filling into prepared crusts. Chill until set (about 1 hour). Top each tart with a dollop of Bourbon Whipped Cream, and dust lightly with cocoa.

Ingredients

— 1 —
CHOCOLATE
PASTRY

p. 23

plus

4 oz. dark chocolate, chopped

4 oz. semisweet chocolate, chopped

1 Tbsp. butter

½ cup heavy cream

1 tsp. vanilla extract

Bourbon Whipped Cream *(p. 256)*

unsweetened cocoa

Baked Until
BUBBLY

The vision of a hot bubbly cobbler baking in the oven always fills me with a sense of excitement. I can hardly keep myself from dipping a spoon into the dish for just a taste!

COBBLERS & CRISPS

Nectarine *and* Tupelo Honey Crisp

MAKES 10 SERVINGS   **HANDS-ON TIME 10 MIN.**   **TOTAL TIME 1 HR., 20 MIN.**

The season's ripest nectarines are the key to this delicious crisp, and the addition of Tupelo honey contributes to its distinctive flavor. Although any sweet white wine may be substituted, late-harvest Riesling perfectly complements the fruit.

1. Preheat oven to 400°. Toss together nectarines and cornstarch in a lightly greased 13- x 9-inch baking dish. Pour wine over fruit, and drizzle with honey. Sprinkle evenly with turbinado sugar. Bake at 400° for 30 minutes or until fruit just begins to brown.

2. Pulse flour, brown sugar, ginger, and salt in a food processor 3 or 4 times until combined. Add marzipan, and pulse 5 or 6 times or until crumbly. Add butter, and pulse 15 times or until mixture resembles coarse meal. Transfer to a bowl; toss in almonds.

3. Sprinkle almond topping over fruit mixture. Bake 25 more minutes or until topping is golden brown. Let stand at least 15 minutes before serving.

Ingredients

12 ripe nectarines, quartered

2 Tbsp. cornstarch

⅔ cup sweet white wine

⅓ cup Tupelo honey or other light honey

¼ cup turbinado sugar

¾ cup all-purpose flour

⅓ cup firmly packed brown sugar

½ tsp. ground ginger

¼ tsp. table salt

2 oz. marzipan (almond paste) (about ⅓ cup), crumbled

½ cup cold butter, cut up

1 cup sliced almonds

Ben's Blueberry Crumble

MAKES 8-10 SERVINGS **HANDS-ON TIME 20 MIN.** **TOTAL TIME 1 HR.**

This is my son Ben's favorite. He always asks for this on his birthday instead of traditional birthday cake. It makes a lot, so I usually send it home with him; it can easily be halved, but I love to have extra … always.

1. Preheat oven to 375°. Toss together blueberries and next 4 ingredients in a large bowl. Spoon mixture into a lightly greased 13- x 9-inch baking dish or 12-inch oven-proof skillet. Dot with butter. Sprinkle Pecan and Oat Crumble over blueberry mixture.

2. Bake at 375° for 40 minutes or until bubbly and golden brown.

Ingredients

3 pt. fresh blueberries

¾ cup sugar

3 Tbsp. all-purpose flour

2 tsp. lemon zest

1 Tbsp. fresh lemon juice

3 Tbsp. cold butter, cut up

Pecan and Oat Crumble (p. 252)

Tip In the spring and early summer, depending on where you live, take advantage of pick-your-own berry farms. This recipe is a great way to use up a lot of blueberries.

Kumquat, Pineapple, *and* Ginger Crisp

MAKES 6 SERVINGS   HANDS-ON TIME 8 MIN.   TOTAL TIME 48 MIN.

This unusual little cobbler will surprise you. What makes it so appealing is the combination of bright, citrusy notes that mingle with flavors of the tropics.

1. Preheat oven to 350°. Combine first 3 ingredients in a medium bowl; cut butter into flour mixture with a pastry blender or fork until crumbly. Stir in coconut.

2. Stir together pineapple, kumquats, ginger preserves, and cornstarch in a medium bowl; spoon into a lightly greased 8-inch square or 9-inch round baking dish. Sprinkle with coconut mixture.

3. Bake at 350° for 40 minutes or until filling is bubbly and topping is lightly browned.

Note: We tested with Dundee ginger preserves.

Ingredients

1 cup all-purpose flour

½ cup firmly packed brown sugar

¼ tsp. table salt

½ cup cold butter, cut up

1 cup sweetened flaked coconut

2 cups chopped fresh pineapple

16 kumquats, quartered and seeded

¾ cup ginger preserves

2 Tbsp. cornstarch

Really Rhubarb-Strawberry Crumble

MAKES 8 SERVINGS   HANDS-ON TIME 9 MIN.   TOTAL TIME 44 MIN.

Rhubarb comes and goes so quickly, be sure to enjoy it while you can. This cobbler makes the most of this extraordinary fruit. Blending it with strawberry preserves enhances its unique flavor and texture.

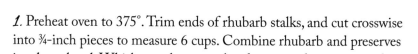

1. Preheat oven to 375°. Trim ends of rhubarb stalks, and cut crosswise into ¾-inch pieces to measure 6 cups. Combine rhubarb and preserves in a large bowl. Whisk together granulated sugar and next 4 ingredients until blended; sprinkle over rhubarb mixture, tossing to coat.

2. Spoon filling into a lightly greased 13- x 9-inch pan or baking dish. Sprinkle Pecan and Oat Crumble over filling. Bake at 375° for 35 minutes or until filling is bubbly and topping is golden brown.

Tip *If you can't get your hands on fresh rhubarb, you can use frozen chopped rhubarb. Just let it thaw completely, drain, and then measure to equal 6 cups.*

Ingredients

1¾ lb. rhubarb stalks

1 (12-oz.) jar strawberry preserves

1 cup granulated sugar

½ cup firmly packed light brown sugar

2 Tbsp. cornstarch

½ tsp. ground cinnamon

¼ tsp. table salt

Pecan and Oat Crumble (p. 252)

Tart Cherry Crisp

MAKES 6-8 SERVINGS   HANDS-ON TIME 25 MIN.   TOTAL TIME 1 HR., 25 MIN.

Bursting with cherries and covered in a buttery almond topping, this crisp is a great way to enjoy the season's first crop.

1. Preheat oven to 350°. Stir together first 3 ingredients in a medium-size nonaluminum saucepan; let stand 15 minutes or until juicy. Bring to a boil over medium heat, stirring constantly. Boil, whisking constantly, 1 minute or until thickened. Remove from heat; stir in almond extract, 1 Tbsp. butter, and ¼ tsp. salt. Pour mixture into a lightly greased 11- x 7-inch baking dish.

2. Stir together flour, brown sugar, cinnamon, and remaining ¼ tsp. salt in a medium bowl. Using your hands, gently combine flour mixture, almonds, and remaining 8 Tbsp. butter until mixture resembles small peas. Sprinkle over cherry mixture.

3. Bake at 350° for 40 minutes or until filling is bubbly and topping is golden brown.

Ingredients

5 cups pitted fresh or frozen tart cherries, thawed

1 cup granulated sugar

3 Tbsp. cornstarch

½ tsp. almond extract

9 Tbsp. butter, softened and divided

½ tsp. table salt, divided

1 cup all-purpose flour

½ cup firmly packed brown sugar

¼ tsp. ground cinnamon

¾ cup sliced almonds, coarsely chopped

Blueberry Buckle

MAKES **10-12 SERVINGS**   HANDS-ON TIME **35 MIN.**   TOTAL TIME **1 HR., 30 MIN.**

Is it cobbler or cake? With this many berries it must be pie—either way it's delectable! The buttermilk batter surrounds the berries, and the cinnamon topping makes the top "buckle" as it bakes.

1. To prepare Batter: Preheat oven to 375°. Beat ½ cup butter and ¾ cup sugar with an electric stand mixer until creamy; add egg, beating until blended.

2. Combine 2 cups flour, baking powder, and salt; add to butter mixture alternately with buttermilk, beating just until blended after each addition. Stir in vanilla. Spread mixture in a greased and floured 13- x 9-inch pan.

3. Stir together blueberries and preserves until blended; spoon over batter in pan.

4. To prepare Cinnamon Topping: Combine ½ cup flour and next 4 ingredients. Cut in 6 Tbsp. butter with a pastry blender until mixture is crumbly. Sprinkle over blueberry mixture. Bake at 375° for 50 minutes. Cool. Serve warm with ice cream, if desired.

* Fresh huckleberries and huckleberry preserves may be substituted for the blueberries and blueberry preserves, if desired.

Ingredients

BATTER

½ cup butter, softened

¾ cup sugar

1 large egg

2 cups all-purpose flour

2 tsp. baking powder

½ tsp. table salt

1 cup buttermilk

2 tsp. vanilla extract

4 cups fresh blueberries*

1 (12-oz.) jar blueberry preserves*

CINNAMON TOPPING

½ cup all-purpose flour

⅓ cup granulated sugar

¼ cup firmly packed light brown sugar

1 tsp. ground cinnamon

¼ tsp. ground nutmeg

6 Tbsp. cold butter, cubed

vanilla ice cream (optional)

Mama's Peach Cobbler

MAKES 8 SERVINGS   **HANDS-ON TIME 16 MIN.**   **TOTAL TIME 56 MIN.**

The first time my mother made this recipe, I was in high school. I thought it might be the best thing I ever tasted. You can make a fancy cobbler, but the simplicity and the flavor of the peaches make it irresistible. The dough forms an almost dumpling-like crust as it bakes. So good!

1. Preheat oven to 375°. Place butter in a 13- x 9-inch baking dish. Bake at 375° for 5 minutes or until butter melts; remove dish from oven.

2. Stir together flour, baking powder, salt, and 1 cup sugar in a large bowl. Add whipping cream, stirring just until dry ingredients are moistened. Pour batter over butter in dish. (Do not stir.)

3. Bring peaches, lemon juice, and remaining 1 cup sugar to a boil in a large saucepan over high heat, stirring constantly; pour over batter. (Do not stir.)

4. Bake at 375° for 40 to 45 minutes or until crust is golden brown. Serve warm with ice cream, if desired.

Ingredients

½ cup butter

1 cup all-purpose flour

1 Tbsp. baking powder

⅛ tsp. table salt

2 cups sugar, divided

1 cup whipping cream

6 cups sliced fresh peaches (8 large)

2 Tbsp. fresh lemon juice

vanilla ice cream (optional)

Latticed Cherry Cobbler

MAKES 8 SERVINGS   HANDS-ON TIME 37 MIN.   TOTAL TIME 2 HR., 22 MIN.

This recipe is really a cross between my two favorite things—pie and cobbler! A traditional lattice tops bright red cherries that peep through. You just can't wait for that first bite of this timeless favorite.

Ingredients

—2—
SIMPLY
PIECRUSTS

p. 12

plus

6 cups pitted
fresh cherries
(about 2¼ lb.)

1 cup granulated sugar

3 Tbsp. cornstarch

2 Tbsp. fresh lemon
juice

⅛ tsp. table salt

3 Tbsp. butter,
cubed

¼ tsp. almond extract

1 large egg,
lightly beaten

1 Tbsp. coarse sugar

1. Prepare Simply Piecrusts through step 1. Preheat oven to 400°. Bring cherries, next 4 ingredients, and ½ cup water to a boil in a medium saucepan, stirring constantly. Boil, stirring constantly, 1 minute. Remove from heat; stir in butter and almond extract.

2. Place 1 dough disk on a lightly floured surface; sprinkle dough lightly with flour. Roll dough into a 13- x 10-inch rectangle. Starting at 1 edge of dough, wrap dough around rolling pin. Place rolling pin over a lightly greased 11- x 7-inch baking dish, and unroll dough over dish. Press dough into dish; trim off excess crust along edges. Brush outer edges of crust lightly with egg; reserve remaining egg. Pour cherry filling into crust.

3. Roll remaining dough disk into an 11- x 10-inch rectangle on a lightly floured surface. Cut dough, parallel to long side, into 10 (1-inch-wide) strips. Arrange strips in a lattice design over filling; gently press ends of strips, sealing to bottom piecrust; crimp edges of crust. Brush lattice with reserved egg; sprinkle with coarse sugar. Place dish on an aluminum foil-lined baking sheet.

4. Bake at 400° on lower oven rack 45 minutes or until juices are thick and bubbly, shielding edges with foil after 35 minutes, if necessary, to prevent excessive browning. Remove from oven to a wire rack, and cool.

Blackberry Cobblers *with* Lemon Cornmeal Crust

MAKES 6 SERVINGS HANDS-ON TIME 15 MIN. TOTAL TIME 1 HR., 30 MIN.

Blackberries grow everywhere down South and are yours for the picking. Plump berries combined with a lemony, cornmeal crust are just divine. These single-serving cobblers thicken as they cool. But no worries if you can't wait—they're equally delicious when eaten right away. Just grab a spoon!

1. Prepare Lemon Cornmeal Piecrust through step 1. Preheat oven to 375°. Toss together blackberries and next 4 ingredients in a large bowl. Spoon about ⅔ cup berry mixture into each of 6 (8-oz.) lightly greased ramekins. Dot with butter.

2. Roll dough to ¼-inch thickness on a lightly floured surface. Cut into 6 rounds using a 3½-inch round cutter. Place dough rounds on top of ramekins. Cut slits in crust to allow steam to escape.

3. Place ramekins on an aluminum foil-lined baking sheet. Bake at 375° for 38 minutes or until bubbly and lightly browned. Remove from oven to a wire rack, and let stand at least 10 minutes before serving.

Ingredients

—1—
LEMON
CORNMEAL
PIECRUST

p.19

plus

4 cups fresh
blackberries

1 cup sugar

¼ cup all-purpose flour

1 Tbsp. fresh lemon
juice

¼ tsp. table salt

3 Tbsp. butter,
cut into small pieces

Fresh Fig *and* Raspberry Cobbler

MAKES 10-12 SERVINGS   HANDS-ON TIME 27 MIN.   TOTAL TIME 1 HR., 29 MIN.

My son Jackson loves Brown Turkey figs. Mix in some fresh raspberries and a sugared biscuit topping, and you have a cobbler that can make a grown man cry.

1. Preheat oven to 425°. Combine first 6 ingredients in a Dutch oven; cook, stirring occasionally, over low heat 15 to 17 minutes or until mixture is bubbly and thick. Remove from heat; discard cinnamon sticks. Stir in vanilla.

2. Pour fig mixture into a lightly greased 13- x 9-inch baking dish; sprinkle with raspberries. Prepare Buttermilk Biscuit Topping through step 1. Drop dough by lightly greased ¼ cupfuls over hot pie filling. (Coat measuring cup with cooking spray after each drop.) Sprinkle tops of biscuits with coarse sugar.

3. Bake at 425° for 18 minutes or until filling is bubbly and biscuits are golden brown. Remove from oven to a wire rack, and let stand 15 minutes before serving.

Tip Make sure to drop the biscuit topping onto hot pie filling so the biscuits cook from the bottom up.

Ingredients

3 lb. figs, stemmed and quartered (8 cups)

1 cup granulated sugar

3 Tbsp. butter

2 Tbsp. cornstarch

¼ tsp. table salt

2 (3-inch) cinnamon sticks

1 tsp. vanilla extract

1 cup fresh raspberries

2 recipes Buttermilk Biscuit Topping *(p. 251)*

3 Tbsp. coarse sugar

Apple-Cranberry Cobbler
with Brown Sugar Crust

MAKES 6 SERVINGS   HANDS-ON TIME 24 MIN.   TOTAL TIME 1 HR., 24 MIN.

Lots of sweet, crisp apples and bright red cranberries combine perfectly in this charming little cobbler. This one is best served at room temperature for the flavors to marry and the topping to crisp up.

1. Prepare Brown Sugar Cookie Topping through step 1; keep chilled. Preheat oven to 375°. Combine apples and next 7 ingredients in a large bowl. Spoon apple mixture into a lightly greased 8-inch square baking dish. Dot with butter.

2. On a lightly floured surface, roll cookie topping into a 9-inch square. Place over apple mixture.

3. Bake at 375° for 30 minutes or until mixture is bubbly and crust is browned. Remove from oven to a wire rack, and cool completely before serving (about 30 minutes).

Ingredients

Brown Sugar
Cookie Topping
(p. 251)

3 cups chopped peeled
Fuji apple (2 large)

2 cups frozen
cranberries,
thawed

1 cup sugar

½ cup chopped toasted
pecans

1 Tbsp. all-purpose
flour

1 Tbsp. orange zest

3 Tbsp. fresh
orange juice

⅛ tsp. table salt

¼ cup butter,
cut up

Roasted Sweet Potato Cobbler

MAKES 6-8 SERVINGS   **HANDS-ON TIME 37 MIN.**   **TOTAL TIME 1 HR., 42 MIN.**

Sweet potatoes and biscuits, two icons of the South, are fashioned into a cobbler to make the best possible treat for cold winter afternoons. What makes this cobbler divine is roasting the sweet potatoes first, which brings out their rich caramel flavor.

Ingredients

3 large sweet potatoes (about 3¼ lb.)

1 Tbsp. canola oil

½ tsp. ground cinnamon

¼ tsp. ground ginger

¼ tsp. ground nutmeg

¼ tsp. table salt

⅓ cup butter, melted

½ cup firmly packed light brown sugar

1 Tbsp. orange zest

3 Tbsp. orange juice

½ cup plus 1 Tbsp. granulated sugar, divided

Buttermilk Biscuit Topping (p. 251)

1. Preheat oven to 400°. Peel sweet potatoes, and cut into 1-inch chunks. Place sweet potatoes in a large bowl; drizzle with oil, tossing to coat. Stir together cinnamon, ginger, nutmeg, and salt; sprinkle over potatoes, tossing to coat. Spread sweet potatoes in a single layer on an aluminum foil-lined baking sheet.

2. Bake at 400° for 30 minutes or until tender, stirring after 20 minutes. Return sweet potatoes to large bowl; drizzle with melted butter, tossing to coat. Add brown sugar, orange zest, orange juice, and ½ cup granulated sugar; toss gently to coat. Spoon sweet potato mixture into a lightly greased 8-inch square baking dish. Reduce oven temperature to 350°.

3. Prepare Buttermilk Biscuit Topping through step 1. Drop by spoonfuls over sweet potato mixture, and sprinkle with remaining 1 Tbsp. granulated sugar. Bake at 350° for 35 minutes or until filling is bubbly and topping is golden brown.

Individual Sweet Potato Cobblers

Divide sweet potato mixture evenly between 6 (4-inch) ramekins. Spoon dough evenly over tops; sprinkle with **1 Tbsp. sugar.** Bake at 400° for 20 to 25 minutes or until lightly browned on top.

Sugar Plum Cobbler

MAKES 6-8 SERVINGS   HANDS-ON TIME 23 MIN.   TOTAL TIME 2 HR., 23 MIN.

When I was seven, our neighbor two doors up had a magnificent plum tree. Most summers it would be loaded with ripe red plums. We would eat them sitting in the grass under the tree, the sticky red juice running down our chins, and then wash our hands with water from the hose when we had eaten our fill.

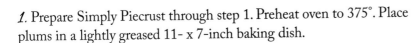

1. Prepare Simply Piecrust through step 1. Preheat oven to 375°. Place plums in a lightly greased 11- x 7-inch baking dish.

2. Stir together brown sugar, next 3 ingredients, and ½ cup granulated sugar in a small bowl; sprinkle over plums. Drizzle with lemon juice, and dot with butter.

3. Roll dough to ⅛-inch thickness on a lightly floured surface. Cut into 11 rounds using a 3-inch round cutter. Place dough rounds, slightly overlapping, on top of plums; brush dough with egg, and sprinkle with remaining 1 Tbsp. granulated sugar. Place dish on an aluminum foil-lined baking sheet.

4. Bake at 375° for 50 minutes or until fruit is tender and pastry is lightly browned.

Ingredients

—1—
SIMPLY
PIECRUST

p. 12

plus

2¾ lb. ripe red plums, quartered (12 large)

½ cup firmly packed dark brown sugar

⅓ cup cornstarch

½ tsp. ground cinnamon

⅛ tsp. table salt

½ cup plus 1 Tbsp. granulated sugar, divided

3 Tbsp. fresh lemon juice

¼ cup butter, cut up

1 large egg, lightly beaten

Plum-Cinnamon Roll Cobbler

MAKES 12 SERVINGS   **HANDS-ON TIME 1 HR., 2 MIN.**   **TOTAL TIME 1 HR., 19 MIN.**

This cobbler is not your average run-of-the-mill fruit pie; it's tart and sweet with an unexpectedly showy cinnamon roll crust.

Ingredients

FILLING

⅓ cup butter

8 large very ripe plums, chopped

1½ cups granulated sugar

1 cup sweetened dried cranberries or dried cherries

1 tsp. orange zest

¼ cup fresh orange juice

CINNAMON ROLL

2¼ cups all-purpose flour

¼ cup granulated sugar

2¼ tsp. baking powder

¾ tsp. table salt

¾ cup cold butter, cut up

⅔ cup whipping cream

⅔ cup firmly packed light brown sugar

3 Tbsp. butter, melted

1 tsp. ground cinnamon

1. To prepare Filling: Preheat oven to 425°. Melt butter in a large skillet over medium-high heat. Add plums, granulated sugar, and cranberries; cook, stirring often, 10 minutes or until plums are tender and mixture thickens. Remove from heat; stir in orange zest and juice. Spoon mixture into a lightly greased 13- x 9-inch baking dish.

2. To prepare Cinnamon Roll: Stir together first 4 ingredients in a large bowl. Cut ¾ cup butter into flour mixture with a pastry blender or fork until crumbly. Add cream, stirring just until dry ingredients are moistened. Turn dough out onto a lightly floured surface, and knead 4 or 5 times. Roll dough into a 12-inch square on a lightly floured surface.

3. Stir together brown sugar, melted butter, and cinnamon in a small bowl; spread over dough, leaving a ½-inch border. Roll up dough, starting at 1 long side; pinch seam to seal. Cut roll into 12 (1-inch) slices. Place slices in a single layer on top of plum mixture.

4. Bake at 425° for 17 minutes or until cinnamon rolls are golden.

Mocha Fudge Cobbler

MAKES 8-10 SERVINGS   HANDS-ON TIME 5 MIN.   TOTAL TIME 1 HR., 5 MIN.

This is a great lazy Sunday afternoon indulgence. Simple pantry ingredients combine to make a rich fudgy cobbler that's so easy and quick.

1. Preheat oven to 350°. Stir together first 3 ingredients, ¾ cup granulated sugar, and 2 Tbsp. cocoa in a medium bowl. Stir together milk, oil, and vanilla; add to flour mixture, stirring until dry ingredients are moistened. Spread batter into a lightly greased 2-qt. baking dish.

2. Stir together brown sugar, remaining ½ cup granulated sugar, and remaining ¼ cup cocoa in a small bowl; sprinkle over batter in pan. Using a spoon, gently drizzle hot coffee over brown sugar mixture, being careful not to disturb layers. (Do not stir.)

3. Bake at 350° for 35 to 40 minutes or until a cake layer forms on top and springs back when lightly touched. Remove from oven to a wire rack, and cool 25 minutes. Serve warm with whipped cream or ice cream, if desired.

Ingredients

1 cup all-purpose flour

2 tsp. baking powder

¼ tsp. table salt

1¼ cups granulated sugar, divided

¼ cup plus 2 Tbsp. unsweetened cocoa, divided

½ cup milk

⅓ cup vegetable oil

1 tsp. vanilla extract

½ cup firmly packed light brown sugar

1½ cups hot brewed coffee

whipped cream or ice cream (optional)

Hot to HANDLE

If you've ever had the lucky pleasure of eating a homemade fried pie or hand pie, then you know how amazingly good they can be. Yummy filling tucked inside a tender crust. It's pie in its humblest form.

HAND PIES & FRIED PIES

Strawberries *and* Cream Mini Pies

MAKES 6 SERVINGS   HANDS-ON TIME 25 MIN. TOTAL TIME 4 HR., 31 MIN. PLUS 1 DAY FOR HOMEMADE CRÈME FRAÎCHE

These amazing little pies can be made the day before and chilled until ready to serve.

1. Prepare Simply Piecrust through step 1. Preheat oven to 425°. Roll dough to ⅛-inch thickness on a lightly floured surface. Sprinkle with 1 Tbsp. sugar; gently roll sugar into crust. Cut into 6 rounds using a 4-inch round cutter.

2. Invert 6 (6-oz.) custard cups several inches apart on a baking sheet. Coat outsides of cups with cooking spray. Place each piecrust round, sugared side up, on a custard cup; press into a bowl shape. Prick piecrust with a fork.

3. Bake at 425° for 10 minutes or until lightly browned. Cool on custard cups 5 minutes. Carefully remove piecrust shells from custard cups; transfer to a wire rack, and cool completely (about 20 minutes).

4. Arrange about half of whole strawberries in piecrust shells (use enough to cover bottom of shells). Cut remaining strawberries in quarters.

5. Combine cornstarch, quartered strawberries, and remaining ¾ cup sugar in a medium-size heavy saucepan, tossing to coat. Bring to a simmer over medium heat, stirring constantly, and mashing strawberries with back of a spoon. Cook, stirring constantly, 1 minute or until thickened. Spoon warm strawberry mixture over whole strawberries in shells. Chill at least 4 hours.

6. Beat Homemade Crème Fraîche at high speed with an electric mixer until stiff peaks form. Serve with pies.

Ingredients

—1—
SIMPLY PIECRUST

p. 12

plus

¾ cup plus 1 Tbsp. sugar, divided

3 cups small fresh strawberries, hulled

2 Tbsp. cornstarch

1 cup Homemade Crème Fraîche *(p. 259)*

Sunny Nectarine Pies

MAKES 5 SERVINGS   HANDS-ON TIME 45 MIN.   TOTAL TIME 4 HR., 18 MIN.

The taste of summer is packed in these tiny pies. Select ripe nectarines; when mashed, they produce juices essential in making a succulent filling.

Ingredients

—— 1 ——
SIMPLY
PIECRUST

p. 12

plus

7 small nectarines, divided (2 lb.)

1 cup sugar

3 Tbsp. cornstarch

3 Tbsp. butter

⅛ tsp. table salt

1 Tbsp. fresh lemon juice

garnish: crème fraîche and mint leaves

1. Prepare Simply Piecrust through step 1. Preheat oven to 400°. Roll dough to ⅛-inch thickness on a lightly floured surface. Cut into 5 rounds using a 7-inch round cutter, rerolling as needed. Fit 1 dough round into each of 5 (4- to 4½-inch) pie pans; fold edges under, and crimp. Line each pastry with aluminum foil, and fill with pie weights or dried beans.

2. Bake at 400° for 10 minutes. Remove weights and foil; bake 8 more minutes or until lightly browned. Remove from oven to a wire rack, and cool completely (about 30 minutes).

3. Peel 3 nectarines, and cut in half. Remove and discard pits. Mash nectarine halves with a fork or potato masher to measure about 1 cup.

4. Stir together mashed nectarines, sugar, next 3 ingredients, and ½ cup water in a medium saucepan. Bring to a boil, and cook, stirring constantly, 2 minutes or until thickened. Pour into a large bowl; cool 30 minutes.

5. Peel remaining 4 nectarines, if desired, and cut into ¼-inch-thick slices to measure about 3 cups; toss with lemon juice. Gently fold nectarine slices into cooked nectarine mixture. Spoon in prepared crusts. Cover and chill 3 hours or until set.

Peach Fried Pies

MAKES 14 SERVINGS   HANDS-ON TIME 33 MIN.   TOTAL TIME 2 HR., 9 MIN.

A warm fried peach pie is just about as Southern as you can get. Some recipes are based on dried peach slices, but I like to use fresh-from-the-orchard peaches.

1. Prepare Fried Pie Pastry as directed. Stir together peach and next 6 ingredients in a medium saucepan. Bring to a boil over medium-high heat, stirring constantly. Boil, stirring constantly, 1 minute or until thickened. Remove from heat; cool completely (about 1 hour).

2. Roll dough to ⅛-inch thickness on a lightly floured surface. Cut into 14 rounds using a 4-inch round cutter, rerolling scraps as necessary.

3. Spoon 1 Tbsp. peach mixture in center of each pastry circle; moisten edges with water. Fold pastry in half, pressing edges to seal using a fork dipped in flour.

4. Pour oil to depth of 2 inches into a Dutch oven; heat to 375°. Fry pies, in batches, 3 to 4 minutes or until golden brown, turning occasionally. Drain on paper towels; sprinkle with powdered sugar.

Tip *To save time, make the pastry, and let it chill while the peach filling cools.*

Ingredients

—1—
FRIED PIE PASTRY
p. 15

plus

1 cup peeled and chopped fresh peach (1 medium)

2 Tbsp. granulated sugar

1 Tbsp. brown sugar

1 Tbsp. cornstarch

1 Tbsp. butter

1 tsp. fresh lemon juice

⅛ tsp. ground cinnamon

vegetable oil

powdered sugar

Blueberry Fried Pies

MAKES 14 SERVINGS **HANDS-ON TIME 30 MIN.** **TOTAL TIME 2 HR., 21 MIN.**

I like to keep these pies assembled and frozen and just fry a few at a time when I don't want to make them all at once.

1. Prepare Fried Pie Pastry as directed. Combine blueberries and next 3 ingredients in a small saucepan. Bring to a boil over medium heat, stirring constantly. Boil, stirring constantly, 2 minutes or until thickened. Remove pan from heat; cool completely (about 30 minutes).

2. Roll dough to ⅛-inch thickness on a lightly floured surface. Cut into 14 rounds using a 4-inch round cutter, rerolling as needed.

3. Spoon 2 tsp. blueberry mixture into center of each circle; moisten edges with water. Fold pastry in half, pressing edges to seal using a fork dipped in flour. Freeze 15 minutes.

4. Pour oil to depth of 2 inches into a Dutch oven; heat to 375°. Fry pies, in batches, 1 to 2 minutes on each side or until golden brown. Drain on paper towels; sprinkle with powdered sugar.

Ingredients

— 1 —
FRIED PIE PASTRY

p. 15

plus

1 cup fresh blueberries

½ cup granulated sugar

2 Tbsp. cornstarch

1 tsp. fresh lemon juice

vegetable oil

powdered sugar

Pretty Pocket Pies

MAKES 6 SERVINGS **HANDS-ON TIME 31 MIN.** **TOTAL TIME 1 HR., 14 MIN.**

Use your favorite jam or preserves—but homemade is unbeatable!

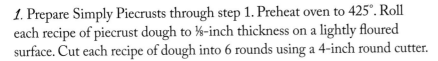

1. Prepare Simply Piecrusts through step 1. Preheat oven to 425°. Roll each recipe of piecrust dough to ⅛-inch thickness on a lightly floured surface. Cut each recipe of dough into 6 rounds using a 4-inch round cutter.

2. Place 6 rounds 2 inches apart on a parchment paper-lined baking sheet. Spoon 1½ Tbsp. preserves in center of each round; moisten edges with water. Top pies with remaining rounds of dough; press edges together with a fork to seal. Cut slits in top for steam to escape.

3. Bake at 425° for 15 minutes or until golden brown. Stir together sugar and cinnamon; sprinkle over warm pies.

Above and beyond Instead of cutting dough into rounds, try cutting it into squares, triangles, or ovals to give some variety to your pocket pies.

Ingredients

—2—
SIMPLY
PIECRUSTS

p. 12

plus

parchment paper

9 Tbsp. blueberry or
raspberry preserves

2 Tbsp. sugar

¼ tsp. ground cinnamon

Homemade Applesauce Hand Pies

MAKES 24 SERVINGS   HANDS-ON TIME 1 HR., 6 MIN.   TOTAL TIME 2 HR., 20 MIN.

These pies are baked, not fried, for a tender, flaky crust. You can make the applesauce ahead of time and chill it until you're ready to assemble and bake pies.

1. Prepare Cream Cheese Piecrusts through step 2. Combine apples, next 8 ingredients, and ¾ cup sugar in a large heavy 8-qt. stockpot; cook over medium-high heat, stirring often, 45 minutes or until apples are tender and juices thicken. Reduce heat, and cook, stirring often, 16 more minutes, mashing any large pieces with a spoon. Remove from heat, and cool 45 minutes. Remove and discard cinnamon stick.

2. Preheat oven to 375°. Roll 1 recipe of piecrust dough to ⅛-inch thickness on a lightly floured surface. Cut into 12 circles using a 4-inch round cutter, rerolling as needed.

3. Place circles on a parchment paper-lined baking sheet; moisten edges of dough with water. Spoon about 1 Tbsp. applesauce into center of each circle; fold over, pressing edges together with a fork to seal. Repeat procedure with remaining recipe of piecrust dough and applesauce.

4. Stir together remaining 3 Tbsp. sugar and ground cinnamon in a small bowl. Brush tops of pies with whipping cream; sprinkle with cinnamon-sugar. Bake at 375° for 15 minutes or until golden brown. Serve warm or at room temperature.

Ingredients

— 2 —
CREAM
CHEESE
PIECRUSTS
p.15

plus

6 large Golden
Delicious apples,
peeled and quartered

¾ cup apple cider

½ tsp. lemon zest

1½ tsp. fresh
lemon juice

¼ tsp. table salt

¼ tsp. ground
cardamom

¼ tsp. ground nutmeg

⅛ tsp. ground cloves

1 (3-inch)
cinnamon stick

¾ cup plus 3 Tbsp.
sugar, divided

parchment paper

¼ tsp. ground cinnamon

2 Tbsp. whipping cream

Chocolate-Cherry Turnovers

MAKES 9 **TURNOVERS**   HANDS-ON TIME **13 MIN.**   TOTAL TIME **31 MIN.**

*My Uncle David made these merry little turnovers.
He would always serve them with a French accent
and require you to eat them with your pinky extended.*

1. Preheat oven to 400°. Microwave preserves and 1 Tbsp. water in a
medium-size microwave-safe bowl at HIGH 30 seconds or until preserves
melt. Stir in dried cherries. Cool completely (about 8 minutes). Stir in
chocolate chunks.

2. Roll puff pastry into a 12- x 12-inch square on a lightly floured surface.
Cut pastry into 9 (4-inch) squares. Spoon cherry mixture evenly into
center of each square, leaving a 1-inch border; brush edges of rectangles
with egg. Fold each square diagonally over filling. Press edges together
with a fork to seal. Cut 2 small slits in top of each turnover for steam
to escape. Brush tops of turnovers with egg; place on a parchment
paper-lined large baking sheet.

3. Bake at 400° for 15 to 18 minutes or until golden brown. Stir together
powdered sugar, whipping cream, and vanilla; drizzle over turnovers.
Serve warm.

Ingredients

⅔ cup cherry preserves

1 cup dried cherries

1 cup chocolate chunks

1 frozen puff
pastry sheet,
thawed

1 large egg,
lightly beaten

parchment paper

1 cup powdered sugar

2 Tbsp. whipping cream

½ tsp. vanilla extract

Spiced Fruit *and* Brie Phyllo Turnovers

MAKES 18 TURNOVERS   HANDS-ON TIME 35 MIN.   TOTAL TIME 50 MIN.

Sugar and spice, dried fruit with Brie, and a splash of brandy are wrapped up together in crispy, buttery phyllo. Now that is cause for celebrating any day!

Ingredients

½ cup apple cider

¼ cup granulated sugar

¼ cup firmly packed dark brown sugar

½ tsp. ground cinnamon

⅛ tsp. ground allspice

⅛ tsp. ground nutmeg

1¼ cups dried fruit bits*

2 Tbsp. brandy

1 (8-oz.) Brie round

6 frozen phyllo sheets, thawed

½ cup butter, melted

parchment paper

1. Preheat oven to 375°. Stir together first 6 ingredients in a large cast-iron skillet; cook over medium-low heat, stirring often, 5 minutes or until sugar dissolves. Stir in dried fruit, and cook 10 minutes or until fruit is tender, stirring occasionally. Remove from heat; stir in brandy.

2. Remove rind from Brie, if desired, and cut round into 18 wedges. Place 1 phyllo sheet on a flat work surface. (Keep remaining phyllo covered with a damp towel to prevent drying out.) Cut sheet lengthwise into 3 (12- x 5-inch) strips. Brush strips with melted butter; fold each strip in half lengthwise to form 3 (12- x 2½-inch) strips, and brush with butter.

3. Place 1 Brie wedge and about 1½ tsp. fruit mixture at 1 end of each strip; fold 1 corner of phyllo over fruit to form a triangle. Continue folding back and forth into a triangle to end of strip.

4. Place triangles, seam side down, on parchment paper-lined baking sheets, and brush with butter. Repeat procedure with remaining phyllo, butter, Brie, and fruit mixture.

5. Bake at 375° for 15 minutes or until golden.

* The package of dried fruit bits we used for testing included a mix of raisins, apples, apricots, peaches, plums, and cherries.

Salted Caramel Pecan Tassies

MAKES 24 TASSIES **HANDS-ON TIME 16 MIN.** **TOTAL TIME 1 HR.**

Salted caramel has become an obsession. These little gems with toasted pecans and cream cheese crusts make it even better.

1. Prepare Cream Cheese Piecrust through step 2. Preheat oven to 400°. Roll dough to ⅛-inch thickness on a floured surface. Cut into 24 rounds using a 2½-inch round cutter, rerolling as needed. Press rounds into 2 (12-cup) miniature muffin pans, forming cups.

2. Bake at 400° for 11 minutes or until lightly browned. Cool in pans on wire racks 10 minutes. Remove from pans to wire racks, and cool completely (about 15 minutes).

3. Combine caramels, cream, and butter in a medium saucepan; cook over low heat, stirring often, 3 minutes or until caramels melt. Remove from heat; stir in pecans.

4. Spoon mixture evenly into prepared piecrusts, and cool completely (about 10 minutes). Sprinkle with coarse sea salt.

Ingredients

— 1 —
CREAM
CHEESE
PIECRUST

p.15

plus

20 caramels

4 tsp. heavy cream

2 tsp. butter

1 cup chopped toasted pecans

¼ tsp. coarse sea salt

Mini Bananas Foster Pies

MAKES 6 PIES   HANDS-ON TIME 28 MIN.   TOTAL TIME 3 HR., 8 MIN.

Be ready with fork in hand to enjoy the gooey goodness of these pies before they melt!

Ingredients

— 1 —
SHORTBREAD
COOKIE
PIECRUST
p. 24

plus

2½ cups vanilla
ice cream,
softened

¼ tsp. ground cinnamon

¼ cup butter

½ cup firmly packed
dark brown sugar

3 medium-size
ripe bananas,
peeled and cut
into ¼-inch slices

1 Tbsp. banana liqueur

1 Tbsp. dark rum

1. Preheat oven to 350°. Prepare Shortbread Cookie Piecrust through step 1. Press crumb mixture into 6 (4- to 4½-inch) pie pans.

2. Bake at 350° for 8 to 10 minutes or until lightly browned. Remove from oven to a wire rack, and cool completely (about 30 minutes).

3. Stir together ice cream and cinnamon in a medium bowl. Spoon mixture evenly into prepared piecrusts. Freeze at least 2 hours or until firm.

4. Melt butter in a medium skillet over medium heat. Add brown sugar, stirring until sugar dissolves. Add bananas, and cook 1 minute. Remove skillet from heat, and carefully stir in banana liqueur and rum. Away from heat, carefully ignite banana mixture with a match; keep away from heat until flames subside. Cook over medium heat 1 minute. Remove from heat, and cool 10 minutes. Spoon warm bananas and syrup over pies, and serve immediately.

Tip These dreamy little pies are best if you prepare them through step 3, and freeze very well. Then when you spoon the warm banana mixture over them, they won't melt as suddenly.

Chocolate Chess Pie Bites

MAKES 24 SERVINGS   HANDS-ON TIME 8 MIN.   TOTAL TIME 1 HR., 3 MIN.

These sweetie pies are great for picnics, tailgating, and family reunions. They travel well and can be whipped up in a jiffy.

1. Prepare Simply Piecrust through step 1. Preheat oven to 350°. Roll dough into a 14-inch circle on a lightly floured surface. Cut into 24 rounds using a 2½-inch round cutter. Press rounds into 2 lightly greased (12-cup) miniature muffin pans, forming cups.

2. Microwave butter and chocolate in a large microwave-safe bowl at MEDIUM (50% power) 1½ minutes or until melted and smooth, stirring at 30-second intervals. Cool 5 minutes. Whisk sugar, vanilla, salt, and egg into chocolate mixture until smooth. Spoon into prepared piecrusts, filling three-fourths full.

3. Bake at 350° for 20 minutes or until filling is set. Cool in pans on a wire rack 10 minutes. Remove from pans to wire rack; cool completely (about 20 minutes).

Ingredients

—1—
SIMPLY
PIECRUST

p. 12

plus

¼ cup butter

1 (1-oz.) semisweet
chocolate baking square

½ cup sugar

½ tsp. vanilla extract

pinch of table salt

1 large egg

Individual Ambrosia Pies

MAKES **6 SERVINGS**   HANDS-ON TIME **37 MIN.**   TOTAL TIME **5 HR., 55 MIN.**

*Southerners love any excuse to serve ambrosia—
Easter, Christmas, New Year's—it doesn't matter.
This petite version of a Southern classic is loaded with
pecans, coconut, and oranges.*

Ingredients

2
GRAHAM
CRACKER
PIECRUSTS
p. 27

plus

1 cup drained
canned crushed
pineapple in juice

1½ cups sweetened
flaked coconut

⅓ cup fresh lemon juice

2 large navel oranges,
sectioned*

1 (14-oz.)
can sweetened
condensed milk

1 cup chopped toasted
pecans, divided

2 cups heavy cream

3 Tbsp. sugar

garnish: orange zest

1. Preheat oven to 350°. Prepare Graham Cracker Piecrusts through step 1, pressing crumb mixture into 6 (4- to 4½-inch) pie pans. Bake at 350° for 8 minutes or until lightly browned. Remove from oven to a wire rack, and cool completely (about 20 minutes).

2. Press pineapple between paper towels. Stir together pineapple, coconut, next 3 ingredients, and ¾ cup pecans in a large bowl.

3. Beat cream until foamy; gradually add sugar, beating until stiff peaks form. Fold into pineapple mixture.

4. Spoon mixture into prepared piecrusts. Cover and chill at least 4 hours. Sprinkle with remaining ¼ cup toasted pecans.

* 1 (11-oz.) can mandarin oranges, drained, may be substituted.

Little Chocolate Brownie Meringue Pies

MAKES **4 SERVINGS**   HANDS-ON TIME **22 MIN.**   TOTAL TIME **1 HR., 2 MIN.**

A rich chocolate brownie covered with soft, billowy meringue is utterly perfect harmony.

1. Preheat oven to 350°. Coat 4 (4- to 4½-inch) pie pans with cooking spray; line bottoms of pans with parchment paper. Coat paper with cooking spray.

2. Beat sugar and next 6 ingredients at medium speed with an electric mixer 4 minutes. Stir in chocolate morsels. Pour batter into prepared pans.

3. Bake at 350° for 20 minutes. (Brownies will not be done.) Spoon or pipe Mile-High Meringue onto pies in a decorative pattern. Bake 20 more minutes or until brownies are done and meringue is golden brown. Serve warm or at room temperature.

Tip Dutch process cocoa can be found next to the regular unsweetened cocoa powder, but the two aren't interchangeable. Dutch process cocoa imparts a smoother flavor and darker color.

Ingredients

parchment paper

1 cup sugar

½ cup all-purpose flour

½ cup butter, softened

⅓ cup Dutch process cocoa

1 tsp. vanilla extract

¼ tsp. table salt

2 large eggs

1 cup semisweet chocolate morsels

Mile-High Meringue (p. 255)

German Chocolate Pies

MAKES 12 PIES   HANDS-ON TIME 48 MIN.   TOTAL TIME 3 HR., 13 MIN.

I always have to hide one of these pies for later because they disappear like magic. The chocolate crust combined with a creamy German chocolate filling is irresistible.

1 (5-oz.) can evaporated milk

½ cup granulated sugar

¼ cup firmly packed light brown sugar

¼ cup butter

2 large egg yolks

½ cup chopped toasted pecans

1 tsp. vanilla extract

1 cup sweetened flaked coconut, toasted

⅓ cup finely chopped German chocolate

1. Prepare 2 recipes of Chocolate Pastry dough through step 1. Preheat oven to 400°.

2. Roll each recipe of dough to ⅛-inch thickness on a lightly floured surface. Cut each recipe of dough into 6 rounds using a 4-inch round cutter. Press rounds into a (12-cup) muffin pan, forming cups. Freeze 10 minutes or until firm.

3. Bake at 400° for 12 to 15 minutes or until set. Cool in pan on a wire rack 10 minutes; remove from pan to wire rack, and cool completely (about 15 minutes).

4. Cook evaporated milk and next 4 ingredients in a heavy 2-qt. saucepan over medium heat, stirring constantly, 3 to 4 minutes or until butter melts and sugar dissolves. Cook, stirring constantly, 10 more minutes or until mixture is bubbly and reaches a pudding-like thickness.

5. Remove pan from heat; stir in pecans, vanilla, and ½ cup coconut. Transfer mixture to a bowl. Let stand, stirring occasionally, 45 minutes or until cooled. Spoon filling evenly into prepared shells; sprinkle with chopped chocolate and remaining ½ cup coconut.

Banana Caramel Pie Poppers

MAKES 12 SERVINGS   HANDS-ON TIME 10 MIN.   TOTAL TIME 1 HR.

A little pop of banana caramel nirvana is awaiting you in every bite. I bet you can't eat just one.

1. Prepare Simply Piecrust through step 1. Preheat oven to 425°.

2. Roll dough into a 16- x 12-inch rectangle on a lightly floured surface. Cut into 12 (4-inch) squares. Place 1 tsp. cream cheese and 1 banana slice onto each square, and sprinkle each with 1 tsp. toffee bits.

3. Bring 4 corners of each square to center, and pinch to form a pouch. Press edges to seal. Place 1 popper in each cup of a lightly greased muffin pan; sprinkle evenly with coarse sugar.

4. Bake at 425° for 12 to 14 minutes or until golden brown. Cool in pan on a wire rack 10 minutes. Remove poppers from pan. Serve warm with Caramel Sauce.

Tip *If you're really pressed for time, you could use store-bought caramel sauce. It won't be quite as divine, but still very delicious.*

Ingredients

— 1 —
SIMPLY
PIECRUST

p. 12

plus

¼ cup cream cheese,
softened

1 large banana,
cut into 12
(½-inch-thick) slices

¼ cup toffee bits

1 Tbsp. coarse sugar

Caramel Sauce
(p. 264)

Pie
APLENTY

*If you are blessed with lots of friends and family,
slab pies are just the ticket. They boast generous helpings and
are easy to serve. No special pans required, just big appetites.*

SLAB PIES

Persimmon Pudding Pie
with Orange Glaze

MAKES 8-10 SERVINGS   HANDS-ON TIME **10 MIN.**   TOTAL TIME **1 HR., 10 MIN.**

Persimmons are an old-timey fruit that ripens in the South during fall. This down-home pudding pie has a delightful flavor that will surprise you.

1. Prepare Sweet Pastry through step 1. Preheat oven to 375°. Cut Sweet Pastry dough log into ¼-inch-thick slices; arrange slices over bottom of a lightly greased 13- x 9-inch pan. Press slices together to cover bottom of pan.

2. Peel persimmons, and cut in half. Remove and discard pits. Process persimmon halves in a food processor until smooth, stopping to scrape down sides as needed.

3. Combine persimmon pulp, sugar, and eggs in a large bowl; beat at medium speed with an electric mixer 2 minutes. Stir together buttermilk and cream. Combine flour and next 5 ingredients; add to persimmon mixture alternately with buttermilk mixture, beginning and ending with flour mixture. Add melted butter and vanilla; beat just until blended. Pour over prepared crust.

4. Bake at 375° for 1 hour or until set. Serve warm with Orange Glaze.

Tip *To speed the ripening process, freeze the fruit overnight or until solid. Thaw the persimmons; when soft, they will be sweeter and less astringent.*

Ingredients

—1—
SWEET
PASTRY
p. 20

plus

4 ripe persimmons
(1 lb.)

1½ cups sugar

3 large eggs

1¼ cups buttermilk

¼ cup heavy cream

1 cup all-purpose flour

1 tsp. baking powder

1 tsp. baking soda

1 tsp. ground cinnamon

¼ tsp. table salt

¼ tsp. ground nutmeg

¼ cup butter,
melted

2 tsp. vanilla extract

Orange Glaze
(p. 268)

Sweet Cherry *and* Nectarine Slab Pie

MAKES **10-12 SERVINGS**   HANDS-ON TIME **34 MIN.**   TOTAL TIME **3 HR., 54 MIN.**

Fresh cherries and nectarines are a match made in heaven. Envelop them in a crispy crust, and it's the ultimate summer pie.

Ingredients

3
SIMPLY
PIECRUSTS
p. 12

plus

2 lb. nectarines
(about 5 medium),
sliced

2 cups fresh cherries,
pitted

1 cup granulated sugar

¼ cup cornstarch

2 Tbsp. almond liqueur
or amaretto liqueur*

⅛ tsp. table salt

1 large egg,
lightly beaten

2 Tbsp. turbinado sugar

1. Prepare all 3 recipes of Simply Piecrust through step 1, dividing dough into 2 equal parts, and forming each part into a square before chilling. (Each square will contain 1½ recipes dough.)

2. Preheat oven to 375°. Roll 1 portion of dough into a 14- x 14-inch rectangle on a lightly floured surface; slide a large baking sheet under dough. Invert a 12-inch square pan onto dough, centering pan on dough. Lift baking sheet, and invert dough into pan, pressing dough into bottom and up sides of pan; trim off excess piecrust along edges.

3. Toss together nectarines and next 5 ingredients in a large bowl; spoon into prepared crust.

4. Roll remaining square of dough into a 13- x 13-inch rectangle on a lightly floured surface; cut piecrust diagonally into 1-inch-wide strips. Arrange strips in a lattice design over filling; gently press ends of strips, sealing to bottom piecrust. Brush with egg; sprinkle with turbinado sugar.

5. Bake at 375° for 50 minutes or until crust is golden brown and filling is bubbly. Cool completely on a wire rack (about 2 hours).

* ½ tsp. almond extract may be substituted.

Almond-Raspberry Meringue Pie

MAKES 12 SERVINGS   HANDS-ON TIME 33 MIN.   TOTAL TIME 4 HR., 31 MIN.

A sweet almond layer spread over the crust makes a wonderful platform for the fresh raspberries and creamy, cloudlike meringue.

1. Prepare both recipes of Simply Piecrust through step 1, combining dough and forming into a rectangle before chilling.

2. Preheat oven to 400°. To prepare Almond Filling: Process all ingredients in a food processor until smooth. Roll dough into a 17- x 12-inch rectangle on a lightly floured surface; transfer dough to a 15- x 10-inch jelly-roll pan, pressing dough into bottom and up sides of pan. Trim dough to top of pan. Line pastry with aluminum foil, and fill with pie weights or dried beans.

3. Bake at 400° for 20 minutes. Remove weights and foil. Spread Almond Filling over prepared crust. Bake at 400° for 18 minutes or until golden brown. Cool completely on a wire rack (about 1 hour).

4. Preheat oven to 325°. To prepare Raspberry Filling: Stir together first 4 ingredients and ¼ cup water in a medium saucepan; bring to a boil over medium heat, stirring constantly. Boil, stirring constantly, 1 minute or until thickened. Remove from heat; stir in 1 Tbsp. butter. Pour Raspberry Filling over Almond Filling in prepared crust.

5. Prepare Mile-High Meringue. Spread meringue over warm filling, sealing edges. Bake at 325° for 20 minutes or until meringue is lightly browned. Cool completely on a wire rack (about 2 hours). Cut into squares.

Ingredients

2
SIMPLY
PIECRUSTS
p. 12

plus

ALMOND FILLING

¼ cup sugar

3 Tbsp. butter, softened

1 Tbsp. all-purpose flour

⅛ tsp. table salt

1 (7-oz.) tube marzipan (almond paste), crumbled

1 large egg

RASPBERRY FILLING

4 cups fresh raspberries

1 cup sugar

¼ cup cornstarch

1 Tbsp. lemon juice

1 Tbsp. butter

Mile-High Meringue (*p. 255*)

Cranberry-Pear Slab Pie

MAKES 10-12 SERVINGS   HANDS-ON TIME 45 MIN.   TOTAL TIME 2 HR., 30 MIN.

Dried cranberries and toasted walnuts are added at the end to give this fruit-laden pie some tartness and crunch.

1. Prepare all 3 recipes of Simply Piecrust through step 1, dividing dough into 2 equal parts, and forming each part into a rectangle before chilling. (Each rectangle will contain 1½ recipes dough.) Preheat oven to 375°.

2. Combine first 5 ingredients and 1 cup sugar in a large saucepan; cook over medium heat, stirring occasionally, 5 minutes or until cranberry skins begin to split. Combine brandy and cornstarch, stirring until smooth. Stir into pear mixture. Bring to a boil over medium heat, whisking constantly. Boil, whisking constantly, 1 to 1½ minutes or until thickened. Remove from heat; stir in dried cranberries and walnuts.

3. Roll 1 portion of dough into a 17- x 12-inch rectangle on a lightly floured surface; transfer dough to a 15- x-10-inch jelly-roll pan, pressing dough into bottom and up sides of pan, allowing edges of dough to extend over sides of pan. Spoon pear mixture into prepared crust.

4. Roll remaining portion of dough into a 16- x 11-inch rectangle on a lightly floured surface; slide a large baking sheet under dough. Slide dough onto pie filling; fold edges under, and crimp, sealing to bottom piecrust. Cut 15 circular openings in top for steam to escape; brush with egg. Stir together cinnamon and remaining 2 Tbsp. sugar; sprinkle over piecrust.

5. Bake at 375° for 43 to 45 minutes or until crust is golden brown. Cool 10 minutes before serving.

Ingredients

— 3 —
SIMPLY PIECRUSTS
p. 12

plus

2¼ lb. firm, ripe Bartlett pears, peeled and sliced

2 cups fresh cranberries

1 Tbsp. orange zest

¾ cup fresh orange juice

⅛ tsp. table salt

1 cup plus 2 Tbsp. sugar, divided

¼ cup brandy

1 Tbsp. cornstarch

1 cup sweetened dried cranberries

1 cup chopped toasted walnuts

1 large egg, lightly beaten

½ tsp. ground cinnamon

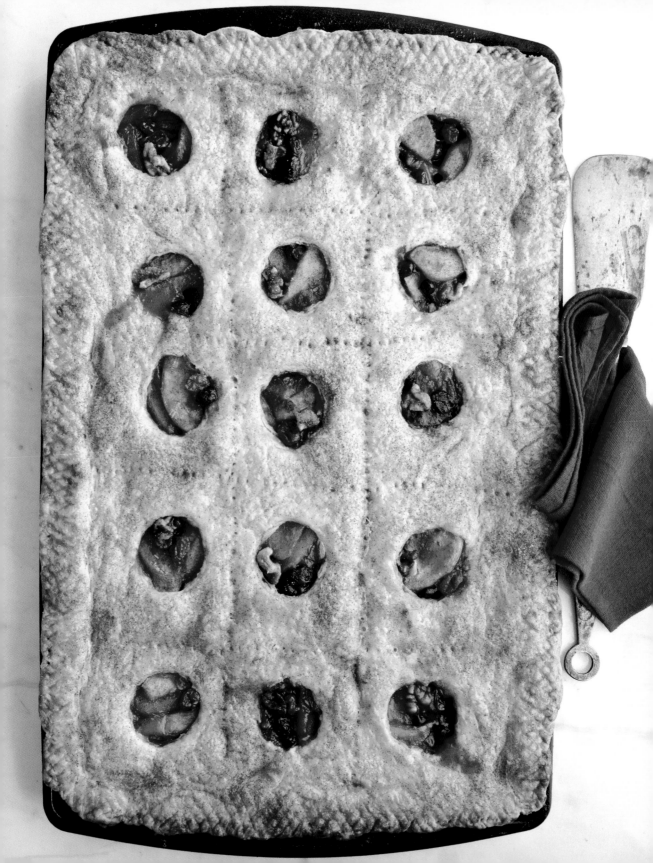

Chunky Chocolate-Cherry Pie

MAKES 12 SERVINGS   HANDS-ON TIME 21 MIN.   TOTAL TIME 3 HR., 11 MIN.

Chunks of chocolate and sweet, juicy cherries buried under a soft, sweet crust could only be better if served with a glass of cold milk.

1. Combine cherries, cornstarch, and 1⅓ cups sugar in a medium saucepan over medium heat; bring to a boil. Boil, stirring constantly, 2 minutes or until thickened. Remove from heat, and cool completely (about 1 hour). Stir in ¼ tsp. almond extract.

2. Preheat oven to 350°. Stir together flour, baking soda, and salt in a small bowl. Beat butter, 1½ cups sugar, and remaining ½ tsp. almond extract in a large bowl at medium speed with an electric mixer until fluffy. Add eggs, 1 at a time, beating just until blended after each addition. Gradually add flour mixture, beating at low speed just until blended. Spread two-thirds of dough in bottom of a lightly greased 13- x 9-inch baking dish.

3. Spoon cherry mixture over dough, and sprinkle with chocolate chunks. Drop remaining one-third of dough by tablespoonfuls onto cherry mixture; sprinkle with remaining 2 Tbsp. sugar.

4. Bake at 350° for 50 minutes or until golden brown. Cool at least 1 hour before serving.

Ingredients

5 cups fresh or frozen pitted tart red cherries, thawed and drained

¼ cup cornstarch

3 cups sugar, divided

¾ tsp. almond extract, divided

2½ cups all-purpose flour

1 tsp. baking soda

⅛ tsp. table salt

1 cup butter, softened

2 large eggs

1 (12-oz.) package chocolate chunks

Rum-Raisin Pie

MAKES **12 SERVINGS** HANDS-ON TIME **45 MIN.** TOTAL TIME **4 HR., 30 MIN.**

A luscious spiced autumn pie is so rich and comforting. Serve it warm with a plentiful dollop of fresh whipped cream.

1. Prepare both recipes of Cream Cheese Piecrust through step 2, dividing dough into 2 equal parts, and forming each part into a rectangle before chilling.

2. Combine raisins and rum in a small saucepan; bring to a boil over medium heat. Remove from heat; cool 30 minutes. Drain raisins, reserving 1 Tbsp. rum.

3. Preheat oven to 400°. Roll 1 rectangle of dough into a 15- x 11-inch rectangle on a lightly floured surface. Transfer dough to a 13- x 9-inch pan, pressing in bottom and up sides of pan. Freeze 10 minutes or until firm.

4. Beat butter and sugars at medium speed with an electric mixer until blended. Add 4 eggs and next 3 ingredients, beating at low speed until blended. Stir in raisins and reserved 1 Tbsp. rum; pour into prepared piecrust.

5. Roll remaining rectangle of dough into a 14- x 10-inch rectangle on a lightly floured surface. Starting at 1 edge of dough, wrap dough around rolling pin. Place rolling pin over pan, and unroll dough over filling, sealing to bottom piecrust. Brush piecrust with egg, and sprinkle with coarse sugar.

6. Bake at 400° for 35 minutes or until crust is golden brown. Remove from oven to a wire rack; cool completely (about 2 hours). Serve with Whipped Cream.

Ingredients

— 2 —
CREAM
CHEESE
PIECRUSTS
p. 15

plus

2 cups raisins

1 cup dark rum

½ cup butter, softened

1 cup granulated sugar

1 cup firmly packed light brown sugar

5 large eggs, lightly beaten

½ cup sour cream

¼ tsp. table salt

¼ tsp. ground cinnamon

2 Tbsp. coarse sugar

Whipped Cream *(p. 256)*

Tiramisù Slab Pie

MAKES 16 SERVINGS   HANDS-ON TIME 18 MIN.   TOTAL TIME 2 HR., 58 MIN.

My daughter, Katie, loves tiramisù; we are always trying new versions. This is a simple recipe that lets all the wonderful flavors we love come through and allows for generous servings.

1. Preheat oven to 350°. Prepare Vanilla Wafer Piecrust through step 1. Press crumb mixture into a 13- x 9-inch baking dish. Bake at 350° for 10 to 12 minutes or until golden brown. Remove from oven to a wire rack, and cool completely (about 30 minutes).

2. Beat cream cheese and powdered sugar at medium speed with an electric mixer until creamy. Add mascarpone cheese; beat at low speed until blended. Add Marsala, beating until blended. Spoon mixture over prepared crust, spreading to edges; sprinkle with dark chocolate. Spoon Coffee Whipped Cream over chocolate, spreading evenly. Cover and chill at least 2 hours or until firm. Cut into squares.

Above and beyond For a more elegant presentation, wait to top with Coffee Whipped Cream until pie is chilled and cut into squares. Then dollop with cream, and sprinkle with grated chocolate and coffee beans.

Ingredients

— 1 —
VANILLA WAFER PIECRUST
p. 24

plus

1 (8-oz.) package cream cheese, softened

1⅓ cups powdered sugar

1 (8-oz.) package mascarpone cheese

2 Tbsp. Marsala or coffee liqueur

2 (4-oz.) dark chocolate baking bars, finely chopped

Coffee Whipped Cream (p. 256)

garnish: grated dark chocolate and chopped chocolate-covered coffee beans

Banana Split Pie

MAKES 12 SERVINGS   HANDS-ON TIME 17 MIN.   TOTAL TIME 4 HR., 57 MIN.

Grown-up kids and pint-size kids alike love this pie. It has the fun surprise of malted milk balls hidden in the filling. Dress it up with all your favorite toppings, and don't forget the cherry on top!

1. Preheat oven to 350°. Prepare Sandwich Cookie Piecrust through step 1; press mixture into bottom of a lightly greased 13- x 9-inch pan. Bake at 350° for 10 minutes. Remove from oven to a wire rack, and cool completely (about 30 minutes).

2. Beat cream cheese at medium speed with an electric mixer until fluffy. Gradually add powdered sugar and malted milk powder, beating until blended. Fold in malted milk balls and 2 cups whipped topping. Spread over prepared crust. Cover and freeze 4 to 24 hours.

3. Spread remaining whipped topping over pie. Toss together bananas and pineapple in a small bowl; arrange over top of pie. Heat hot fudge topping according to package directions; drizzle over fruit, and top with sprinkles. Top with cherries.

Ingredients

— 1 —
SANDWICH
COOKIE
PIECRUST
p. 23

plus

1 (8-oz.) package cream cheese, softened

1½ cups powdered sugar

1 cup malted milk powder

1 cup chocolate-covered malted milk balls

1 (12-oz.) container frozen whipped topping, thawed and divided

2 ripe bananas, chopped

2 cups diced fresh pineapple

hot fudge topping

chocolate candy sprinkles

1 cup whole red maraschino cherries (with stems)

Frozen Strawberry-Lemonade Pie

**MAKES 8 SERVINGS   HANDS-ON TIME 20 MIN.   TOTAL TIME 1 HR., 7 MIN.
PLUS 1 DAY FOR FREEZING**

*Tart-sweet lemonade blended with creamy strawberry sorbet
is the perfect way to end the hot, humid days of summer.
A knife dipped in hot water makes slicing this a breeze.*

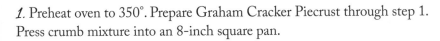

1. Preheat oven to 350°. Prepare Graham Cracker Piecrust through step 1.
Press crumb mixture into an 8-inch square pan.

2. Bake at 350° for 10 to 12 minutes or until lightly browned. Remove
from oven to a wire rack, and cool completely (about 30 minutes).

3. Beat cream cheese at medium speed with an electric mixer until
smooth. Gradually add lemonade concentrate, beating until blended.
Stir in sorbet.

4. Spoon mixture into prepared piecrust. Freeze 8 to 24 hours or until firm.

5. Let stand at room temperature 10 minutes before slicing.

Tip *This is an easy recipe to double, if you're serving a crowd. Just
prepare twice the amount, and freeze in a 13- x 9-inch baking dish.*

Ingredients

— 1 —
GRAHAM
CRACKER
PIECRUST
p. 27

plus

1 (8-oz.) package
cream cheese,
softened

½ cup thawed frozen
lemonade concentrate

1 pt. strawberry sorbet,
softened

garnish: sliced fresh
strawberries and
whipped cream

Frozen Creamy Lime *and* Blueberry Pie

MAKES 16 SERVINGS   HANDS-ON TIME 44 MIN.   TOTAL TIME 7 HR., 54 MIN. PLUS 1 DAY FOR HOMEMADE CRÈME FRAÎCHE

Ingredients

── 1 ──
SHORTBREAD
COOKIE
PIECRUST
p. 24

plus

1⅓ cups sugar

1 Tbsp. lime zest

1 cup fresh lime juice

8 large egg yolks

1 cup cold butter, cut up

2 tsp. chopped fresh mint

¼ tsp. table salt

Blueberry Syrup

Homemade
Crème Fraîche
(p. 259)

garnish: fresh
blueberries and fresh
mint sprigs

1. Preheat oven to 350°. Prepare Shortbread Cookie Piecrust through step 1. Press crumb mixture into a 13- x 9-inch baking dish. Bake at 350° for 10 to 12 minutes or until golden brown. Cool completely on a wire rack.

2. Bring sugar, zest, and juice to a boil in a heavy nonaluminum 3-qt. saucepan over medium-high heat. Remove from heat, and gradually whisk one-fourth hot juice mixture into egg yolks; add egg yolk mixture to remaining hot juice mixture, whisking constantly until well blended. Cook over medium heat, whisking constantly, 10 minutes or until thick.

3. Add butter, in 6 batches, whisking constantly until butter melts and mixture is well blended after each addition. Remove from heat, and pour into a bowl. Stir in mint and salt. Place heavy-duty plastic wrap directly on warm custard (to prevent a film from forming); chill 4 hours.

4. Prepare Blueberry Syrup. Beat Homemade Crème Fraîche in a large bowl at medium speed with an electric mixer until stiff peaks form; fold in chilled lime curd. Spread mixture over prepared crust. Spoon Blueberry Syrup by teaspoonfuls over lime mixture; swirl gently with a knife. Freeze 2 hours or until firm. Cut into squares.

Blueberry Syrup

Combine *1 cup fresh blueberries, 3 Tbsp. sugar,* and *2 Tbsp. water* in a small saucepan; bring to a boil over medium heat. Cook, stirring occasionally, 5 minutes or until mixture slightly thickens. Remove from heat. Press blueberry mixture through a wire-mesh strainer using the back of a spoon to squeeze out juice into a small bowl; discard solids. Cool completely (about 30 minutes). Chill until ready to use.

Frozen Lemon *and* Berries Pie

MAKES 12 SERVINGS   HANDS-ON TIME 31 MIN.   TOTAL TIME 6 HR., 36 MIN.

Choose your favorite summer fruit and berries to layer in this rich lemon custard frozen pie.

1. To prepare Graham and Granola Piecrust: Preheat oven to 350°. Process granola in a food processor until coarsely ground. Add graham cracker crumbs, sugar, and melted butter; pulse 5 or 6 times or until combined. Press onto bottom of a 13- x 9-inch baking dish. Bake at 350° for 10 minutes or until lightly browned. Cool completely on a wire rack (about 20 minutes).

2. To prepare Frozen Lemon Custard: Whisk together sugar, cornstarch, and salt in a medium saucepan. Gradually whisk in cream, milk, and eggs; bring to a boil over medium heat, whisking constantly. Boil, whisking constantly, 1 to 1½ minutes or until thickened. Remove pan from heat; stir in lemon zest and juice. Pour into a bowl. Place heavy-duty plastic wrap directly on warm custard (to prevent a film from forming); chill 1 hour.

3. Spread half of chilled custard over prepared crust. Sprinkle with cherries, blackberries, and blueberries. Spread with remaining half of custard. Cover and freeze at least 4 hours or until firm.

4. Let stand at room temperature 5 minutes before serving. Cut into squares; top with strawberries.

Ingredients

GRAHAM AND GRANOLA PIECRUST

2 cups plain granola without raisins

1 cup graham cracker crumbs

⅓ cup sugar

5 Tbsp. butter, melted

FROZEN LEMON CUSTARD

1 cup sugar

¼ cup cornstarch

⅛ tsp. table salt

2 cups heavy cream

1 cup milk

2 large eggs

2 tsp. lemon zest

1 cup fresh lemon juice

plus

1 cup fresh cherries, pitted

1 cup fresh blackberries or raspberries

1 cup fresh blueberries

3 cups sliced fresh strawberries

Mississippi Mud Pie

MAKES 12 SERVINGS   **HANDS-ON TIME 14 MIN.**   **TOTAL TIME 39 MIN.**

This little quote from Erma Bombeck says it all…"Seize the moment. Remember all those women on the Titanic *who waved off the dessert cart."*

1. Preheat oven to 325°. To prepare Brownie Batter: Microwave butter and chocolate squares in a medium-size microwave-safe bowl at HIGH 1½ minutes or until melted and smooth, stirring at 30-second intervals. Cool 5 minutes. Stir in granulated sugar, vanilla, and eggs until blended. Add flour and ½ tsp. salt, stirring just until blended.

2. Spread Brownie Batter into a lightly greased 13- x 9-inch pan. Bake at 325° for 20 minutes or just until top is set. Remove from oven; immediately sprinkle with marshmallows and 1 cup chocolate morsels.

3. To prepare Frosting: Combine butter, evaporated milk, and cocoa in a medium saucepan; cook over medium heat until butter melts. Cook, stirring constantly, 2 minutes or until mixture slightly thickens.

4. Remove from heat; whisk in powdered sugar, vanilla, and ¼ tsp. salt until smooth. Immediately pour over marshmallows and chocolate morsels. Sprinkle with toasted pecans and remaining 1 cup chocolate morsels.

Ingredients

BROWNIE BATTER

¾ cup butter

4 (1-oz.) unsweetened chocolate baking squares

¾ cup granulated sugar

1 tsp. vanilla extract

2 large eggs, lightly beaten

1 cup all-purpose flour

½ tsp. table salt

2 cups miniature marshmallows

2 cups semisweet chocolate morsels, divided

FROSTING

½ cup butter

½ cup evaporated milk

⅓ cup unsweetened cocoa

1 (16-oz.) package powdered sugar

1 tsp. vanilla extract

¼ tsp. table salt

1 cup pecans, toasted

Peanut Butter
and Jam Pie Bars

MAKES 24 SERVINGS   HANDS-ON TIME 15 MIN.   TOTAL TIME 1 HR., 5 MIN.

Homemade jam or preserves make a delicious filling for these decadent pie bars. If you don't have any homemade jam on hand, buy your favorite—or call your grandmother or great-aunt, and see if you can raid her pantry!

1. Preheat oven to 350°. Beat peanut butter and ⅓ cup butter at medium speed with an electric mixer until creamy. Add granulated sugar and ½ cup brown sugar, beating well. Add eggs and vanilla; beat until blended. Combine baking powder, 1¼ cups flour, and ½ tsp. salt; stir into peanut butter mixture just until blended. Press mixture onto bottom of a 15-x 10-inch jelly-roll pan. Bake at 350° for 20 minutes or until edges are lightly browned. Cool 5 minutes; spread with jam.

2. Combine peanuts, remaining 1 cup brown sugar, 1 cup flour, ½ cup butter, and ¼ tsp. salt in a small bowl with a pastry blender until crumbly. Sprinkle topping over jam. Bake at 350° for 30 minutes or until topping is lightly browned.

Tip *Served warm, these bars are a gooey, sweet, and salty treat to eat with a fork. Cooled completely, they slice cleanly and can be eaten out of hand.*

Ingredients

½ cup creamy
peanut butter

½ cup plus ⅓ cup butter,
softened and divided

½ cup granulated sugar

1½ cup firmly
packed brown sugar,
divided

2 large eggs

1 tsp. vanilla extract

1 tsp. baking powder

2¼ cups all-purpose
flour, divided

¾ tsp. table salt, divided

2 cups of your favorite
homemade jam

½ cup chopped
dry-roasted peanuts

Chocolate Chip and Toffee Pie

MAKES 16 SERVINGS   HANDS-ON TIME 20 MIN.   TOTAL TIME 2 HR.

Served warm in square slabs, this chocolaty pie is ooey gooey, making it just the thing if you are seeking comfort food. A scoop of vanilla ice cream atop each serving makes any day an occasion to celebrate.

Ingredients

1
GRAHAM
CRACKER
PIECRUST

p. 27

plus

1 cup butter, softened

3 large eggs

2 tsp. vanilla extract

1 cup granulated sugar

1 cup firmly packed dark brown sugar

1½ cups all-purpose flour

½ tsp. table salt

2 cups semisweet chocolate morsels

2 cups toffee bits, divided

1 cup milk chocolate morsels

1 cup pecans, chopped and toasted

vanilla ice cream (optional)

1. Preheat oven to 350°. Prepare Graham Cracker Piecrust through step 1. Press crumb mixture in bottom of a lightly greased 13- x 9-inch baking dish. Bake at 350° for 10 minutes or until lightly browned.

2. Beat butter, eggs, and vanilla at high speed with an electric mixer until creamy. Add sugars; beat at medium speed until blended. Add flour and salt, beating just until blended. Stir in semisweet chocolate morsels and 1 cup toffee bits. Spread into prepared crust.

3. Bake at 350° for 38 to 40 minutes or just until set. (The center will be gooey and will set as it cools.) Remove from oven to a wire rack, and cool completely (about 1 hour).

4. Microwave milk chocolate morsels in a small glass bowl at HIGH 30 to 45 seconds or until melted and smooth, stirring after 30 seconds. Drizzle melted chocolate over pie; sprinkle with toasted pecans and remaining 1 cup toffee bits. Serve warm with ice cream, if desired.

Top
THAT

Every now and then you want something over the top,
something simply indulgent. Pie all by itself is a "special treat"
as my granddaughter calls it. But add an exceptional
topping or sauce, and your pie becomes extraordinary.

PIE TOPPINGS

Buttermilk Biscuit Topping

Buttermilk Biscuit Topping

MAKES 15 BISCUITS   HANDS-ON TIME **11 MIN.**   TOTAL TIME **29 MIN.**

I can't resist a biscuit topping—crunchy on top and soft underneath. If you aren't in the mood for piecrust, this is the answer.

1. Preheat oven to 425°. Combine flour and sugar in a large bowl; cut butter into flour mixture with a pastry blender or fork until crumbly. Add buttermilk, stirring just until dry ingredients are moistened.

2. Drop dough by lightly greased ¼ cupfuls over hot pie filling in a lightly greased baking dish. (Coat measuring cup with cooking spray after each drop.)

3. Bake at 425° for 18 minutes or until golden brown.

Ingredients

1½ cups self-rising flour

1 Tbsp. sugar

6 Tbsp. cold butter, cut up

¾ cup buttermilk

Brown Sugar Cookie Topping

MAKES **TOPPING FOR (8-INCH) COBBLER**   HANDS-ON TIME **15 MIN.**   TOTAL TIME **45 MIN.**

1. Pulse first 5 ingredients in a food processor 3 or 4 times or until combined. Add butter, and pulse 5 or 6 times or until crumbly. With processor running, gradually add egg, and process until dough forms a ball and pulls away from sides of bowl. Wrap dough in plastic wrap, and chill 30 minutes.

2. Preheat oven to 375°. On a lightly floured surface, roll cookie topping into a 9-inch square. Place over pie filling in an 8-inch square baking dish, fold edges under, and crimp; bake as directed in recipe.

Ingredients

1¼ cups all-purpose flour

¾ cup firmly packed light brown sugar

½ tsp. ground ginger

¼ tsp. ground cinnamon

⅛ tsp. table salt

6 Tbsp. butter

1 large egg

Sugared Piecrust Strips

MAKES 32 STRIPS   HANDS-ON TIME 10 MIN.   TOTAL TIME 25 MIN.

1. Prepare Simply Piecrust through step 1. Preheat oven to 450°. Roll dough to ⅛-inch thickness on a lightly floured surface. Cut into ¾- to 1-inch-wide strips. Place on a lightly greased baking sheet; sprinkle with sugar.

2. Bake at 450° for 5 to 8 minutes or until golden brown. Cool on baking sheet 10 minutes.

Pecan *and* Oat Crumble

MAKES 4½ CUPS   HANDS-ON TIME 5 MIN.   TOTAL TIME 5 MIN.

1. Stir together first 5 ingredients in a medium bowl. Cut butter into oat mixture with a pastry blender or fork until crumbly. Stir in pecans.

2. Sprinkle mixture evenly over fruit filling before baking as directed in recipe.

* Toasted coconut, chopped toasted almonds, chopped toasted walnuts, or chopped toasted hazelnuts may be substituted.

Ingredients

— 1 —
SIMPLY
PIECRUST

p.12

plus

2 Tbsp. sugar

Ingredients

1 cup firmly packed brown sugar

1 cup uncooked regular oats

¾ cup all-purpose flour

⅛ tsp. table salt

⅛ tsp. nutmeg

½ cup cold butter, cut up

1 cup coarsely chopped pecans, toasted*

Pecan and Oat Crumble

Mile-High Meringue

Mile-High Meringue

MAKES TOPLING FOR (9-INCH) PIE **HANDS-ON TIME 9 MIN.** **TOTAL TIME 9 MIN.**

1. Preheat oven to 325°. Beat first 3 ingredients at high speed with an electric mixer just until foamy. Gradually add sugar, 1 Tbsp. at a time, beating until stiff peaks form and sugar dissolves (about 2 to 4 minutes).

2. Spread meringue over hot filling, sealing edges. Bake at 325° for 15 to 20 minutes or until meringue is lightly browned.

Brown Sugar Mile-High Meringue
Substitute *¼ cup firmly packed light brown sugar* and *¼ cup granulated sugar* for the sugar in the recipe.

Ingredients

6 large egg whites

½ tsp. cream of tartar

½ tsp. vanilla extract

½ cup sugar

Marshmallow Meringue

MAKES TOPLING FOR (9-INCH) PIE **HANDS-ON TIME 8 MIN.** **TOTAL TIME 16 MIN.**

1. Preheat oven to 400°. Beat first 3 ingredients at high speed with an electric stand mixer until foamy. Gradually add sugar, 1 Tbsp. at a time, beating just until stiff peaks form and sugar dissolves (2 to 4 minutes).

2. Beat one-fourth of marshmallow crème into egg white mixture; repeat 3 times with remaining marshmallow crème, beating until smooth (about 1 minute).

3. Spread meringue over hot filling, sealing edges. Bake at 400° for 8 to 10 minutes or until meringue is lightly browned.

Ingredients

3 large egg whites

½ tsp. vanilla extract

⅛ tsp. table salt

¼ cup sugar

1 (7-oz.) jar marshmallow crème

Whipped Cream

MAKES 4 CUPS   HANDS-ON TIME 5 MIN.   TOTAL TIME 5 MIN.

Ingredients

2 cups heavy whipping cream

6 Tbsp. powdered sugar

1. Beat whipping cream at high speed with an electric mixer until foamy; gradually add sugar, beating until soft peaks form.

Serve as is or, if desired, stir in ingredient listed in one of the following variations:

Basil: ¼ cup chopped fresh basil

Bourbon: ¼ cup bourbon

Caramel: ½ cup caramel sauce

Chocolate Chip: ½ cup semisweet chocolate mini-morsels

Coffee: 1 Tbsp. instant espresso dissolved in 1 Tbsp. hot water, cooled

Orange: 2 Tbsp. thawed, frozen orange juice concentrate and 1 Tbsp. orange zest

Peppermint: 1 tsp. peppermint extract

Sweet Mint: 2 Tbsp. to ¼ cup chopped fresh mint

Whipped Cream Cheese Topping

MAKES 6 CUPS   HANDS-ON TIME 10 MIN.   TOTAL TIME 10 MIN.

Ingredients

1 (8-oz.) package cream cheese, softened

¾ cup powdered sugar

1 tsp. vanilla extract

⅛ tsp. table salt

2½ cups heavy cream

1. Beat cream cheese, sugar, vanilla, and salt at medium speed with a heavy-duty electric stand mixer, using whisk attachment, until smooth and creamy. Gradually add cream, beating at medium speed until stiff peaks form.

Whipped Cream

Georgia Honey and Cream

Georgia Honey *and* Cream

MAKES 2½ CUPS   HANDS-ON TIME 5 MIN.   TOTAL TIME 35 MIN.

Mountain honey from north Georgia is special. When combined with buttery mascarpone cheese and cream, it makes pie ethereal.

1. Beat all ingredients at medium speed with an electric mixer until soft peaks form. Cover and chill 30 minutes.

Ingredients

1 (8-oz.) package mascarpone cheese, at room temperature

1 cup heavy whipping cream

¼ cup Georgia honey

3 Tbsp. powdered sugar

Pinch of table salt

Homemade Crème Fraîche

MAKES 2 CUPS   HANDS-ON TIME 3 MIN.   TOTAL TIME 3 MIN.
PLUS 1 DAY FOR STANDING

Don't let the name fool you. This is one topping that is effortless to make and goes well with so many pies. It isn't sweet so sometimes I add a tiny bit of sugar to it and whip it slightly with a whisk till it has soft peaks.

1. Combine cream and buttermilk in a sterilized 1-qt. jar or glass container. Cover and let stand at room temperature (about 70°) 8 to 24 hours or until very thick. Stir well.

2. Cover and chill at least 2 hours and up to 10 days.

Ingredients

2 cups heavy cream

¼ cup buttermilk

Make Mine ... à la Mode

MAKES 10–12 SERVINGS   HANDS-ON TIME 15 MIN.   TOTAL TIME 5 HR., 15 MIN. PLUS 1 DAY FOR CHILLING

Ingredients

3 cups half-and-half

1¼ cups powdered sugar

2 large egg yolks

1 (8-oz.) package cream cheese, cubed and softened

2 tsp. vanilla bean paste or vanilla extract

1. Whisk together first 3 ingredients in a large heavy saucepan. Cook over medium heat, whisking constantly, 8 to 10 minutes or until mixture thickens slightly. Remove from heat, and whisk in cream cheese and vanilla bean paste until cheese melts. Cool completely (about 1 hour), stirring occasionally. Place plastic wrap directly on mixture (to prevent a film from forming), and chill 8 to 24 hours.

2. Pour mixture into freezer container of a 1½-qt. electric ice-cream maker, and freeze according to manufacturer's instructions. (Instructions and times will vary.) Transfer ice cream to an airtight container. Freeze 4 hours before serving.

Serve as is or, if desired, stir in ingredient listed in one of the following variations:

Brown Sugar–Cinnamon: ½ cup firmly packed dark brown sugar and 1 tsp. ground cinnamon

Chocolate Fudge Chip: 1 cup hot fudge topping and 1 cup mini-morsels

Coffee: 2 Tbsp. instant espresso dissolved in ¼ cup hot water, cooled

Fresh Coconut Cream: 1 cup fresh coconut or frozen grated coconut, thawed and toasted, and 1 tsp. coconut extract

Ginger: 6 Tbsp. finely chopped crystallized ginger

Honey: ½ cup honey

Maple-Bourbon-Pecan: 1 cup chopped toasted pecans, ½ cup maple syrup, and ¼ cup bourbon or whiskey

Orange: 2 Tbsp. orange zest

Peanut Butter: ¾ cup peanut butter and ½ cup chopped dry-roasted peanuts

Peanut Butter

Honey

Brown Sugar-Cinnamon

Mississippi Mud Sauce

Mississippi Mud Sauce

MAKES **4 CUPS** HANDS-ON TIME **18 MIN.** TOTAL TIME **18 MIN.**

It's a been a tradition at my house for as long as I can remember to pour this warm, fudgy topping over pie and ice cream.

1. Bring cream to a boil in a large heavy saucepan over medium-high heat; reduce heat to low, and simmer. Add chocolate morsels, and stir until melted and smooth. Stir in marshmallow crème and vanilla, stirring constantly until smooth. Serve warm.

Ingredients

1 cup heavy cream

1 (12-oz.) package dark chocolate morsels

1 (7½-oz.) jar marshmallow crème

½ tsp. vanilla extract

Chocolate Ganache

MAKES **ABOUT 1 CUP** HANDS-ON TIME **5 MIN.** TOTAL TIME **5 MIN.**

Ganache just might be the perfect food for chocolate lovers. Serve warm or cold, drizzled or poured. It turns any pie into a chocoholic's dream.

1. Place chocolate morsels in a small bowl. Bring cream to a simmer in a small saucepan over medium heat; pour over chocolate morsels. Let stand 2 minutes. Add butter, whisking until smooth.

Ingredients

⅔ cup semisweet chocolate morsels

½ cup heavy cream

1½ tsp. butter

Caramel Sauce

MAKES 1½ CUPS   HANDS-ON TIME 5 MIN.   TOTAL TIME 20 MIN.

This rich sauce is best served while warm. Pour over and around your pie, and wait for the "oh my goodness" to begin.

Ingredients

1 cup firmly packed light brown sugar

½ cup butter

¼ cup whipping cream

¼ cup honey

1. Bring all ingredients to a boil in a medium saucepan over medium-high heat, stirring constantly; boil, stirring constantly, 2 minutes. Remove from heat, and cool 15 minutes before serving. Store in an airtight container in refrigerator up to 1 week. To reheat, microwave at HIGH 10 to 15 seconds or just until warm; stir until smooth.

Apple Cider Drizzle

MAKES 1 CUP   HANDS-ON TIME 39 MIN.   TOTAL TIME 1 HR., 39 MIN.

It takes a little time to reduce the cider to a syrup, so I generally make extra; if I'm feeling generous, I might even share a jar or two.

Ingredients

4 cups apple cider

½ cup firmly packed light brown sugar

2 Tbsp. butter

1. Bring apple cider to a boil in a large saucepan over medium-high heat. Boil 35 minutes or until reduced to ⅔ cup. Stir in brown sugar and butter; cook, stirring constantly, 2 minutes or until sugar dissolves and mixture is smooth. Remove from heat, and cool 1 hour.

Caramel Sauce

Lemon Curd

Lemon Curd

MAKES **2 CUPS** HANDS-ON TIME **25 MIN.** TOTAL TIME **55 MIN.**

1. Stir together first 4 ingredients in a large saucepan over medium heat, and cook, stirring constantly, until sugar dissolves and butter melts.

2. Gradually whisk about one-fourth of hot sugar mixture into eggs; add egg mixture to remaining hot sugar mixture, whisking constantly. Cook over medium-low heat, stirring constantly, 15 minutes or until mixture thickens and coats a spoon. Remove from heat; cool. Store in an airtight container in refrigerator up to 2 weeks.

Ingredients

2 cups sugar

¼ cup lemon zest

1 cup fresh lemon juice
(about 6 lemons)

½ cup butter,
coarsely chopped

4 large eggs,
lightly beaten

Alabama Custard Cream

MAKES **1½ CUPS** HANDS-ON TIME **13 MIN.** TOTAL TIME **8 HR., 13 MIN.**

With micro dairies on the rise in Alabama, getting fresh milk and cream is pretty easy and worth the effort. This makes a most delicious addition to serve with pie. I like to pour it while warm onto my plate and place my pie on top. Or by all means pour it over the top.

1. Whisk together first 4 ingredients in a medium-size heavy saucepan. Bring to a boil over medium heat, whisking constantly. Boil, whisking constantly, about 5 minutes or until thickened. Remove pan from heat.

2. Whisk egg yolk until thick and pale. Gradually whisk about one-fourth of hot milk mixture into egg yolk; whisk egg mixture into remaining hot milk mixture, whisking constantly. Cook over medium heat, stirring constantly, 2 minutes or until thickened. Remove pan from heat; stir in butter and vanilla bean paste. Pour custard into a bowl. Serve warm, or place plastic wrap directly onto warm custard (to prevent a film from forming), and chill at least 8 hours.

Ingredients

1½ cups milk

½ cup sugar

2 Tbsp. all-purpose
flour

¼ tsp. table salt

1 large egg yolk

2 tsp. butter

½ tsp. vanilla bean paste

Kentucky Bourbon Hard Sauce

MAKES 2¼ CUPS   HANDS-ON TIME 10 MIN.   TOTAL TIME 10 MIN.

If you've ever had hard sauce, you will never forget it, and if you haven't, this is about to change your life. Serve a dollop over warm pie. It's the next best thing to … well, you decide.

1. Beat butter at medium speed with an electric mixer until creamy. Gradually add powdered sugar and bourbon, beating until light and fluffy. Serve immediately, or cover and chill until ready to serve.

Ingredients

1 cup butter, softened

2 cups powdered sugar

3 Tbsp. Kentucky bourbon

Orange Glaze

MAKES ⅔ CUP   HANDS-ON TIME 18 MIN.   TOTAL TIME 48 MIN.

It may be hard to believe something this simple is so good. You may want to make extra because you may find yourself drizzling this over more than pie.

1. Combine orange juice, sugar, and butter, in a small saucepan; bring to a boil over medium heat. Cook 10 minutes or until syrupy and liquid is reduced to ⅔ cup, stirring occasionally. Remove from heat; stir in orange zest. Cool 30 minutes.

Ingredients

½ cup fresh orange juice

⅓ cup sugar

2 Tbsp. butter

1 Tbsp. orange zest

Kentucky Bourbon Hard Sauce

Easy as pie

Whether passed down through generations or bright, shiny, and new, the right tools and equipment make it easy to bake the perfect pie.

1

2

3

4

5

1 BENCH KNIFE
Also called a dough scraper, it has lots of uses. It gives a straight edge when cutting pastry and is great for gently working together some shaggy dough.

2 PIE WEIGHTS
The two most popular kinds of these weights are ceramic and metal, but dried beans work, too. They prevent an unfilled crust from shrinking or falling during baking.

3 PIE PLATES AND PANS
I love my heirloom pie tins for the crispy brown crust they impart and their nostalgic look. However, if I want to be sure the crust is evenly baked, I use a clear glass pie plate so I can see how brown it's getting.

4 SIFTER
A small sifter is perfect for sprinkling a little flour over a work surface and for dusting some powdered sugar or cocoa on the top of a piece of pie.

5 JELLY-ROLL PAN
When baking extra-juicy pies, a rimmed baking sheet is the best way to avoid a messy cleanup. It is also perfect for baking slab pies and for holding several mini tart pans at once.

6 KITCHEN SHEARS
This simple tool is my secret for easily snipping the excess pastry from around the edge of a pie plate.

7 TART AND TARTLET PANS
Look for tart pans with removable bottoms in a variety of shapes and sizes—they are essential for creating beautiful tarts!

8 PIE SERVER
A triangular blade and a bent handle are critical to get down the pie plate edge and under the crust so not a crumb is left behind.

9 COOLING RACK
Both functional and beautiful, a cooling rack allows air to circulate around the pie so it's cool enough to slice.

10 PASTRY WHEEL
This tool makes latticework quicker and prettier, too. I like to run it up against a ruler for the straightest lines.

11 PIE BIRDS
These sweet little birds will never make a chirp, but they will silently let the steam escape from a double-crust pie, preventing spillover.

12 RULER

Precision when rolling pastry to a certain thickness and cutting to the perfect size is so important for even baking and beautiful results.

13 PEELER

A peeler is my secret weapon for making whimsical chocolate curls for the top of a pie.

14 ROLLING PIN

There are so many styles to pick from: with or without handles, tapered or straight, wooden or marble. Just pick one you feel comfortable with—and never put it in the dishwasher!

15 MEASURING SPOONS

Make sure that your measuring spoons are accurate. A little too much salt or too little baking powder can turn your pie into a disaster.

Pure and simple

A pie is a wondrous thing. Starting with just a few seemingly humble ingredients and ending with a little heat from the oven brings to life a dessert that is both nostalgic and divine.

1

BUTTER

NET WT. 4 OZ. (113.4g)

BUTTER

2 BUTTER

3

1. LARD
Lard imparts a lot of flavor and is similar to working with shortening. My favorite crust uses part lard and part butter.

2. BUTTER
An all-butter crust is guaranteed to be flavorful, but working with it can be a bit tricky. Just be sure to keep the dough cool, and don't overmix it.

3. SHORTENING
It's easy to make a flaky, tender crust with shortening. It doesn't melt as fast as butter so it's a little more forgiving.

4. WHOLE WHEAT FLOUR
I like to substitute whole wheat flour for some of the all-purpose flour in a recipe. It gives a nutty, wholesome flavor, without becoming too dense.

5. CAKE FLOUR
If I'm making biscuits or a soft dough, I'll use part cake flour and part all-purpose flour so the crumb turns out tender.

6. ALL-PURPOSE FLOUR
This flour has just enough gluten (protein) to hold together a dough like a piecrust or a cookie. If I want to experiment with other flours, I just mix a bit into my all-purpose flour.

7 MOLASSES
With its intense flavor, molasses gives pie fillings more than just sweetness; its dark richness and acidity make for a deep, truly Southern flavor.

8 GRANULATED SUGAR
Great for mixing into doughs and fillings, granulated sugar gives pies simple sweetness and crunch without distracting from a fruit or cream filling.

9 BROWN SUGAR
Depending on how much I want the flavor to shine through, I use either light

7

8

9

10

or dark brown sugar. Dark brown sugar gives pies a stronger molasses flavor, while light brown gives them just a hint of it.

10 CANE SYRUP

I love baking with cane syrup! I use 100% pure cane syrup for its pure sweet flavor. I mix it into fillings and sometimes drizzle it over a slice of pie or a biscuit.

11 HEAVY CREAM

Brushing heavy cream over a crust before baking helps the crust brown evenly and gives it a matte finish.

12

DEMERARA SUGAR

Also known as turbinado sugar, demerara sugar can be sprinkled over a latticed pie or cobbler to give a bit of a crunch and a little sparkle.

13 BEATEN EGG

When lightly brushed over dough before baking, it seals edges and ensures a shiny, golden brown crust.

Crust Index

Put your own spin on Southern pie! Start from the bottom up with any of these crusts, then add one of my suggested fillings. Just substitute the new crust for the crust listed in the recipe.

SIMPLY PIECRUST

p. 12

Try this crust with:

Brown Turkey Fig Pie 80

Individual Ambrosia Pies 210

Rum-Raisin Pie 230

DEEP SOUTH PIECRUST

p. 12

Try this crust with:

Shoofly Pie 47

Black Skillet Apple Pie 71

Sugar Plum Cobbler 181

COCONUT PIECRUST

p. 19

Try this crust with:

Chocolate Fudge Pie
with Praline Crumble 51

Mocha Mud Pie 117

Frozen Creamy Lime
and Blueberry Pie 238

LEMON CORNMEAL PIECRUST

p. 19

Try this crust with:

Summer Berry Pies 63

Mixed Plum Pie 76

Bridge Club Tart 141

SHORTBREAD COOKIE PIECRUST

p. 24

Try this crust with:

Brown Sugar and Date Tart 129

Fresh Fig and Goat Cheese
Tart 142

Sunny Nectarine Pies 190

VANILLA WAFER PIECRUST

p. 24

Try this crust with:

Red Velvet Pie 85

Caramel-Banana-Walnut Tart 137

Banana Split Pie 234

GRAHAM CRACKER PIECRUST

p. 27

Try this crust with:

Frozen Orange Cream Pie 110

Lemon Pie with Basil
Whipped Cream 89

Sweet Potato Pie with
Marshmallow Meringue 106

CREAM
CHEESE
PIECRUST

p. 15

Try this crust with:
Maple and Black Walnut Pie 56
Butterscotch Pie 109
Latticed Cherry Cobbler 170

RUSTIC
ALMOND
PIECRUST

p. 16

Try this crust with:
Amelia's Egg Custard Pie 39
Classic Cherry Pie 67
Sweet Cherry and Nectarine
Slab Pie 222

CHEDDAR
PIECRUST

p. 16

Try this crust with:
Cider Apple Pie 68
Fresh Peach and Apricot Pie 79
Cranberry-Pear Slab Pie 226

SWEET
PASTRY

p. 20

Try this crust with:
Tart Lemon Chess Pie 43
Rosemary Apple Tart 122
Strawberries and Cream
Mini Pies 189

CHOCOLATE
PASTRY

p. 23

Try this crust with:
Frosty Peppermint Pie 113
Sweetheart Tart 145
Salted Caramel Pecan Tassies 205

SANDWICH
COOKIE
PIECRUST

p. 23

Try this crust with:
Peanut Butter Candy Pie 114
Tuxedo Tart 138
Tiramisù Slab Pie 233

GINGERSNAP
PIECRUST

p. 27

Try this crust with:
Banana Cream Pie 86
Blackberry-Buttermilk Tart 130
Chocolate Chip and Toffee Pie 246

PRETZEL
PIECRUST

p. 28

Try this crust with:
Dark Chocolate Cream Pie 98
Mini Bananas Foster Pies 206
Frozen Strawberry-Lemonade
Pie 237

PHYLLO
PIECRUST

p. 31

Try this crust with:
Mixed Berry Cream Pie 90
Fresh Orange Tart with
Honey-Glazed Pistachios 134

Index

$\mathcal{V}$

$\mathcal{W}$

$\mathcal{Z}$

Metric Equivalents

The information in the following charts is provided to help cooks outside the United States successfully use the recipes in this book. All equivalents are approximate.

EQUIVALENTS FOR DIFFERENT TYPES OF INGREDIENTS

Standard Cup	Fine Powder	Grain	Granular	Liquid Solids	Liquid
	(ex. flour)	*(ex. rice)*	*(ex. sugar)*	*(ex. butter)*	*(ex. milk)*
1	140 g	150 g	190 g	200 g	240 ml
¾	105 g	113 g	143 g	150 g	180 ml
⅔	93 g	100 g	125 g	133 g	160 ml
½	70 g	75 g	95 g	100 g	120 ml
⅓	47 g	50 g	63 g	67 g	80 ml
¼	35 g	38 g	48 g	50 g	60 ml
⅛	18 g	19 g	24 g	25 g	30 ml

LIQUID INGREDIENTS BY VOLUME

¼ tsp =					1 ml
½ tsp =					2 ml
1 tsp =					5 ml
3 tsp =	1 Tbsp =		½ fl oz =		15 ml
	2 Tbsp =	⅛ cup =	1 fl oz =		30 ml
	4 Tbsp =	¼ cup =	2 fl oz =		60 ml
	5⅓ Tbsp =	⅓ cup =	3 fl oz =		80 ml
	8 Tbsp =	½ cup =	4 fl oz =		120 ml
	10⅔ Tbsp =	⅔ cup =	5 fl oz =		160 ml
	12 Tbsp =	¾ cup =	6 fl oz =		180 ml
	16 Tbsp =	1 cup =	8 fl oz =		240 ml
	1 pt =	2 cups =	16 fl oz =		480 ml
	1 qt =	4 cups =	32 fl oz =		960 ml
			33 fl oz =	1000 ml	= 1 l

LENGTH

(To convert inches to centimeters, multiply the number of inches by 2.5.)

1 in =			2.5 cm	
6 in =	½ ft =		15 cm	
12 in =	1 ft =		30 cm	
36 in =	3 ft =	1 yd =	90 cm	
40 in =			100 cm	= 1 m

COOKING/OVEN TEMPERATURES

	Fahrenheit	Celsius	Gas Mark
Freeze Water	32° F	0° C	
Room Temperature	68° F	20° C	
Boil Water	212° F	100° C	
Bake	325° F	160° C	3
	350° F	180° C	4
	375° F	190° C	5
	400° F	200° C	6
	425° F	220° C	7
	450° F	230° C	8
Broil			Grill

DRY INGREDIENTS BY WEIGHT

(To convert ounces to grams, multiply the number of ounces by 30.)

1 oz =	¹⁄₁₆ lb =	30 g
4 oz =	¼ lb =	120 g
8 oz =	½ lb =	240 g
12 oz =	¾ lb =	360 g
16 oz =	1 lb =	480 g

ISBN-13: 978-0-8487-3963-8
ISBN-10: 0-8487-3963-9

Library of Congress Control Number: 2013939091
Printed in the United States of America
First Printing 2013

SOUTHERN LIVING®

Editor: M. Lindsay Bierman
Creative Director: Robert Perino
Managing Editor: Candace Higginbotham
Art Director: Chris Hoke
Executive Editors: Rachel Hardage Barrett, Hunter Lewis, Jessica S. Thuston
Food Director: Shannon Sliter Satterwhite
Senior Food Editor: Mary Allen Perry
Deputy Food Director: Whitney Wright
Test Kitchen Director: Robby Melvin
Recipe Editor: JoAnn Weatherly
Test Kitchen Specialist/Food Styling: Vanessa McNeil Rocchio
Test Kitchen Professionals: Norman King, Pam Lolley, Angela Sellers
Photographers: Robbie Caponetto, Laurey W. Glenn, Melina Hammer, Hector Sanchez
Senior Photo Stylist: Buffy Hargett
Editorial Assistant: Pat York

TIME HOME ENTERTAINMENT INC.

Publisher: Jim Childs
VP, Brand & Digital Strategy: Steven Sandonato
Executive Director, Marketing Services: Carol Pittard
Executive Director, Retail & Special Sales: Tom Mifsud
Director, Bookazine Development & Marketing: Laura Adam
Executive Publishing Director: Joy Butts
Associate Publishing Director: Megan Pearlman
Finance Director: Glenn Buonocore
Associate General Counsel: Helen Wan

OXMOOR HOUSE

Editorial Director: Leah McLaughlin
Creative Director: Felicity Keane
Senior Brand Manager: Daniel Fagan
Senior Editor: Rebecca Brennan
Managing Editor: Elizabeth Tyler Austin

the Southern Pie Book

Editor: Allison E. Cox
Art Director: Claire Cormany
Project Editor: Lacie Pinyan
Senior Designer: J. Shay McNamee
Assistant Directors, Test Kitchen: Julie Christopher, Julie Gunter
Recipe Developers and Testers: Wendy Ball, R.D.; Victoria E. Cox; Tamara Goldis; Stefanie Maloney; Callie Nash; Karen Rankin; Leah Van Deren
Recipe Editor: Alyson Moreland Haynes
Food Stylists: Margaret Monroe Dickey, Catherine Crowell Steele
Photography Director: Jim Bathie
Senior Photographer: Hélène Dujardin
Senior Photo Stylist: Kay E. Clarke
Photo Stylist: Mindi Shapiro Levine
Assistant Photo Stylist: Mary Louise Menendez
Senior Production Manager: Sue Chodakiewicz
Assistant Production Manager: Diane Rose Keener

CONTRIBUTORS

Author: Jan Moon
Compositors: Carol Damsky, Cathy Robbins
Recipe Developers and Testers: Erica Hopper, Tonya Johnson, Kyra Moncrief, Kathleen Royal Phillips
Copy Editors: Donna Baldone, Dolores Hydock
Proofreader: Norma Butterworth-McKittrick
Indexer: Nanette Cardon
Photographer: Becky Luigart-Stayner
Food Stylist: Ana Price Kelly
Photo Stylist: Fonda Shaia
Interns: Morgan Bolling, Megan Branagh, Frances Gunnells, Susan Kemp, Sara Lyon, Staley McIlwain, Jeffrey Preis, Maria Sanders, Julia Sayers